EX   SIVE
EDUCATION

EXPANSIVE
EDUCATION

Teaching learners for the real world

BILL LUCAS, GUY CLAXTON AND ELLEN SPENCER

WITH A FOREWORD BY ARTHUR L COSTA

ACER PRESS AND OPEN UNIVERSITY PRESS

First published 2013

Published in Australia and New Zealand by ACER Press, an imprint of
Australian Council for Educational Research Ltd
19 Prospect Hill Road, Camberwell, Victoria, 3124, Australia
www.acerpress.com.au
sales@acer.edu.au
ISBN: 9781742861104

Published in the United Kingdom by Open University Press
McGraw-Hill Education
McGraw-Hill House
Shoppenhangers Road, Maidenhead
Berkshire, England, SL6 2QL
www.openup.co.uk
enquiries@openup.co.uk
and Two Penn Plaza, New York, NY 10121-2289, USA
ISBN-13: 9780335247554
ISBN-10: 0335247555
eISBN: 9780335247561

Edited by Elisa Webb
Cover design, text design and typesetting by ACER Creative Services
Printed and bound by CPI Group (UK) Ltd, Croydon, CR0 4YY

National Library of Australia Cataloguing-in-Publication data:

Author: Lucas, Bill, author.

Title: Expansive education : teaching learners for the real world / Bill Lucas ; Guy Claxton ;
                     Ellen Spencer ; with a foreword by Arthur C Costa.

ISBN: 9781742861104 (paperback)

Notes: Includes bibliographical references and index.

Subjects: Learning.
                     Teaching.

Other Authors/Contributors:
                     Claxton, Guy, author.
                     Spencer, Ellen, author.

Dewey Number: 370.1523

A catalogue record of this book is available from the British Library

Library of Congress Cataloguing-in-Publication Data
CIP data applied for

Foreword

Language and thinking are intimately related. How we see the world is reflected in the way we talk and write. If we refer to education as 'expansive', it suggests a different view of school from the one that is currently valued by many today. If we choose to use the word 'disposition' rather than 'skill', we are signalling that we value certain habits of mind in action.

In *Don't think of an elephant: know your values and frame the debate*, George Lakoff perfectly encapsulates the importance of language when changing attitudes is the goal:

> *Frames are mental structures that shape the way we see the world.
> As a result, they shape the goals we seek, the plans we make, the
> way we act, and what counts as a good or bad outcome of our
> actions ... To change our frames is to change all of this. Reframing
> is social change ... Reframing is changing the way the public sees
> the world. It is changing what counts as common sense. Because
> language activates frames, new language is required for new
> frames. Thinking differently requires speaking differently.*[1]

Expansive education: teaching learners for the real world by Bill Lucas, Guy Claxton and Ellen Spencer achieves just the kind of reshaping that Lakoff describes. The authors persuade us to reframe the way we see education and at the same time use the language of expansiveness to help activate new ways of thinking about school. In this excellent book there are numerous, convincing reasons as to why we should change things, illuminated by rich resources for helping us to do so. And the book is full of vivid examples of schools, teachers and organisations from around the world that have reframed the way they see education and the positive results that have accrued.

At this time in history there is an international surge, a kind of 'intellectual spring', brought on by the realisation that a country's future in the 21st century and beyond depends on its people's creativity, problem solving, communication and collaboration. This creates new imperatives for education systems.

National ministries of education around the world are adopting expansive approaches to education exemplified by dispositional teaching and learning. And these countries—Finland and Singapore are just two examples mentioned in the book—are also achieving excellent results on conventional test scores. National ministries are beginning to address the significant knowledge, concepts and dispositions needed to understand and act creatively and innovatively on issues of global significance. Those competencies and the dispositions they require include such essentials as:

- investigating the world beyond students' immediate environment
- recognising students' own and others' perspectives
- communicating their ideas effectively with diverse audiences
- translating their ideas and findings into appropriate actions to improve conditions.[2]

These essentials themselves require certain propensities, inclinations or dispositions such as:

- curiosity, wonderment, questioning and problem posing
- taking risks, persisting and striving for accuracy
- empathising with others, collaborating, inhibiting impulse and listening
- thinking flexibly and communicating with clarity both orally and in writing.

It is apparent that if these outcomes are to become the new goals of education, then our views of education, instruction, assessment and the very purposes of school will need to shift. Such mind shifts include:

From knowing right answers to knowing how to behave when answers are not readily apparent

In the past, schools tended to teach, assess and reward convergent thinking and the acquisition of content with a limited range of acceptable answers. Life in the real world, however, demands multiple ways to do something well. A fundamental shift is required from valuing right answers as the purpose for learning, to knowing how to behave when we *don't* know answers—knowing what to do when confronted with those paradoxical, dichotomous, enigmatic, confusing, ambiguous, discrepant and sometimes overwhelming situations which plague our lives. We need to move from valuing knowledge *acquisition* as an outcome to valuing knowledge *production* as an outcome. We want students to learn how to develop a critical stance with their work: inquiring, thinking flexibly and learning from another person's perspective.

As we reframe, we will need to let go of our obsession with acquiring content knowledge as an end in itself, and make room for viewing content as a vehicle for developing broader, more pervasive and complex goals that are identified and substantiated in this book.

From transmitting meaning to constructing meaning

Meaning-making is not a spectator sport. Knowledge is a constructive process rather than a finding. It is not the content that gets stored in memory, but the activity of constructing it that gets stored. Humans don't *get* ideas; they *make* ideas.

As neuroscientists study the processes of learning, they are realising that a constructivist model of learning reflects their best understanding of the brain's natural way of making sense of the world.

Constructivism holds that learning is essentially active. A person learning something new brings to that experience all of their previous knowledge and present mental patterns. Each new fact or experience is assimilated into a living web of understanding that already exists in that person's mind. Learning is neither passive nor simply objective.

Furthermore, meaning-making is not just an individual operation. The learner interacts with others to construct shared knowledge. There is a cycle of internalisation of what is socially constructed as shared meaning, which is then externalised to affect the learner's social participation. Constructivist learning, therefore, is viewed as a reciprocal process in that the individual influences the group and the group influences the individual.[3]

Little or no learning will take place unless the learning environment is trustful and the others who are significant to the learner (parents, teachers, coaches, etc.) model the desired outcomes. One of the greatest distractions to trust is when there is incongruity with how an adult acts and what that adult professes. This suggests that teachers, administrators and parents must learn how to 'walk the talk' through modelling the dispositions of a continuous and inquiring learner.

From external to internal assessment

The earlier Lakoff quotation included the words: 'Our frames shape what counts as a good or bad outcome of our actions'. This implies a need to reframe our language actions, paradigms of assessment and evaluation of educational outcomes. We assess what we value and value what we assess. Evaluation of learning has been viewed as summative measures of how much content a student has retained. It is useful for grading and segregating students into ability groups. It even serves estate agents in fixing home prices in relationship to neighbourhoods' published test scores! But while we wholeheartedly want all students to do as well as they possible can on whatever test they take, such attainment is only part of what they will need to thrive in the real world. And important dispositional goals cannot be assessed using right-answer-oriented measurement techniques.

It's time to move beyond our narrow approach to assessing the acquisition of content, and collect evidence of learning that expands beyond content knowledge. Metacognition is our ability to reflect on how effectively we are handling the problem solving. When we observe students persisting with difficult tasks, overcoming frustration, setting and achieving goals, seeking help, working with others, monitoring and adjusting to changing circumstances while accomplishing their specific goals—these are the metacognitive qualities that are vastly more important, transferrable, life-long-lasting and essential than recalling how to factor a polynomial.

Assessment, therefore, should be neither summative nor punitive. Rather, assessment is a mechanism for providing ongoing feedback to the learner as a necessary part of the spiralling processes of continuous renewal: self-managing, self-monitoring and self-modifying. We must constantly remind ourselves that the ultimate purpose of evaluation is to have students learn to become self-evaluative. If students graduate from our schools still dependent upon others to tell them when they are adequate, good or excellent, then we've missed the whole point of what education is about.

Reframing society, however, is no easy task. Peter Medawar, British biologist, said, 'The human mind treats a new idea the same way the body treats a strange protein; it rejects it'.[4] Trying to change the views of parents, politicians and educators and their subsequent behaviour and language, even with the best possible justification, will necessarily generate in them discomfort. Indeed, some people reading this timely, thoughtful and well-researched book may well find their comfort zones disturbed!

Is the struggle of reframing suggested in *Expansive education: teaching learners for the real world* futile? Are we doomed to the status quo? Certainly not! Human beings are gloriously adaptive. The human brain is amazingly modifiable. And we can all—teachers, parents, educators and politicians—continue to learn, unlearn and act differently. So, what actions should we take?

Start with yourself. Immerse yourself in this book and others of a like mind that are recommended herein. Focus on and attend to the dispositional teaching and learning described.

Use and customise the dispositions described in the book as outcomes for yourself and your institution. Our expectations shape our reality. The preconceptions of students, teachers, administrators and parents have a significant impact on what they perceive to be important in life.

Persist. Repeated, purposeful and focused attention can lead to long-lasting personal change. Such attention shapes our own identity over time. With enough concentrated attention, individual thoughts and acts of the mind become an intrinsic part of an individual's identity: who we are, how we perceive the world and how our brains work.

Join the Expansive Education Network and engage with others in discussions of these dispositions. Minds are best reframed through interaction with others. Pay particular attention to others who may resist or are reluctant to embrace the reframing. They are your friends as they help to sharpen and refine your advocacy.

And, perhaps most importantly, as Mahatma Gandhi said, become a model of the dispositions you value: 'You must be the change you wish to see in the world'.

If we wish for a world that is more compassionate, more cooperative, more thoughtful and more expansive, it must emanate from within each of us.

Arthur L Costa, EdD
Granite Bay, California
Professor Emeritus, California State University, Sacramento and
Co-Founder, Institute for Habits of Mind International

Contents

List of figures and tables

Acknowledgements

We are enormously grateful to the United Kingdom's Comino Foundation for providing financial and moral support to the University of Winchester's Centre for Real-World Learning. This resource has enabled us to create the Expansive Education Network, build alliances with expansive educators and focus on what we believe is an essential direction for education. This book is one direct outcome of their support.

Pioneers in the field

An increasing number of organisations are working in the field of expansive education, many of whom we have not yet established contact with. We would specifically like to acknowledge and thank those that have helped us, explicitly or indirectly, to research and write this book.

Organisations and initiatives

ASDAN, UK
http://www.asdan.org.uk/
Association of Chartered Teachers,
Scotland
http://acts.edublogs.org/
Australian Council for Educational
Research
http://www.acer.edu.au/
Building Learning Power, UK
http://www.
buildinglearningpower.co.uk/
Campaign for Learning, UK
http://www.campaign-for-
learning.org.uk/
Center for the Future of Elementary
Education at Curtis School, USA
http://www.curtiscfee.org/info/

Center on School, Family and
Community Partnerships, USA
http://www.csos.jhu.edu/p2000/
center.htm
Centre for Science Education,
Sheffield Hallam University, UK
http://www.shu.ac.uk/research/
cse/
Comino Foundation, UK
http://www.cominofoundation.
org.uk/
Creativity, Culture and Education,
UK
http://www.
creativitycultureeducation.org/
CUREE (Centre for the Use of
Evidence and Research in

Education), UK
http://www.curee.co.uk/

The Curriculum Foundation, UK
http://www.
curriculumfoundation.org/

The Design and Technology
Association, UK
http://www.data.org.uk/

Eden Project, England
http://www.edenproject.com/

ExpandED Schools, USA
http://www.expandedschools.
org/

Expansive Education Network, UK
http://www.expansiveeducation.
net/

Expansive Learning Network,
Australia
http://expansivelearning.com.au/

Expeditionary Learning, USA
http://elschools.org/

The European framework for key
competences, Belgium
http://ec.europa.eu/education/
lifelong-learning-policy/
key_en.htm

Fieldwork Education, UK
http://www.greatlearning.com/

Hands On Learning, Australia
http://handsonlearning.org.au/

The Institute for Habits of Mind,
USA

http://www.
instituteforhabitsofmind.com/

The International Baccalaureate,
Switzerland
http://www.ibo.org/

International Institute for the
Enhancement of Learning
Potential, Israel
http://en.feuerstein-global.org/
institute

Kestrel, UK
http://www.thinkingschool.co.
uk/

The Leonardo Effect, UK
http://www.leonardoeffect.com/

Learning Futures, UK
http://www.phf.org.uk/landing.
asp?id=368

Learning Network NZ, New
Zealand
http://www.learningnetwork.ac.
nz/

Learning through Landscapes, UK
http://www.ltl.org.uk/

Open Futures, UK
http://www.openfutures.com/

Mastering Learning, USA
http://masteringlearning.com/

Mind Lab, UK
http://www.mindlabuk.com/

Mindset Works, USA
http://www.mindsetworks.com/

Optimise Learning, Singapore
http://www.optimiselearning.com/

The Partnership for 21st Century Skills, USA
http://www.p21.org/

The Philosophy Foundation, UK
http://www.philosophy-foundation.org/

Philosophy4Children, UK
http://www.philosophy4children.co.uk/

Project Zero, USA
http://www.pz.harvard.edu/

QED Foundation, USA
http://qedfoundation.org/

RSA Opening Minds, UK
http://www.rsaopeningminds.org.uk/

SAPERE (Society for the Advancement of Philosophical Enquiry and Reflection in Education), UK
http://www.sapere.org.uk/

SSAT (Specialist Schools and Academies Trust), UK
http://www.ssatuk.co.uk/

Teaching Leaders, UK
http://www.teachingleaders.org.uk/

Tender Bridge, Australia
https://tenderbridge.acer.edu.au/Pages/Public/Home.aspx

Thinking Schools, UK
http://www.thinkingschool.co.uk/resources/thinking-school-links

The 21st Century Learning Alliance, UK
http://www.21stcenturylearningalliance.org/

Visible Thinking, USA
http://www.pz.gse.harvard.edu/visible_thinking.php

Whole Education, UK
http://www.wholeeducation.org/

Widehorizons, UK
http://www.widehorizons.org.uk/

Schools, colleges and universities

Aberdeen University School of Education, Scotland

Australian International School, Singapore

Bankstown Girls' High School, Australia

Bath Spa University School of Education, England

Bay House School, England

Bialik College, Australia

Brighton University School of
Education, England

Center on School, Family, and
Community Partnerships, Johns
Hopkins University, USA

Centre for Science Education at
Sheffield Hallam University,
England

Deakin University, Australia

Eton College, England

Exeter University Cognitive
Education Development Unit,
England

GEMS, Dubai

Harvard Graduate School of
Education, USA

Holy Trinity Primary School,
London, England

Institute of Education, London
University, England

Kites Language School, Argentina

Koulumestari School, Finland

Manchester Metropolitan University
Institute of Education, England

Nayland Primary School, England

Newcastle University Research
Centre for Learning and
Teaching, England

Oxford and Cherwell Valley
College, England

Plymouth University Faculty of
Education, England

RSA Academy, England

St Mary's University College,
Northern Ireland

South-West Wales Centre for
Teacher Education, Wales

Stonefields Primary School, New
Zealand

Toronto University Institute for
Studies in Education, Canada

Waikiki School, USA

Waikato University School of
Education, New Zealand

Winchester University Faculty of
Education, Health and Social
Care, England

Wellington College, England

Wolverhampton University, England

Ynystawe Primary School, Wales

Chapter 1

Widening goals, strengthening minds and creating enquiring teachers

We must remember that intelligence is not enough. Intelligence plus character—that is the goal of true education. The complete education gives one not only power of concentration, but worthy objectives upon which to concentrate

Martin Luther King, Jr

The idea of education that is more than traditional schooling is not new. Ever since statutory education for the majority of children became a reality, thoughtful educators, concerned parents, perceptive employers and enlightened national policy-makers have argued that schools should connect more effectively with the real world. But, too often, such arguments have been polarised, partisan, simplistic and unsupported by evidence.

Recently, there have been some significant shifts in thinking about the global context in which education sits and a much sharper grasp of the research that helps us to understand why different kinds of schooling produce different results.

We have coined the expression 'expansive education' to describe an approach to education which is increasingly being taken up internationally. In *Expansive education: teaching learners for the real world*, we explore the purpose of education in a rapidly changing world. In this context, we analyse the thinking and science behind the idea of expansive education and describe some of the pioneering work which has been and is being undertaken in schools. Drawing on both research and practice, we offer a theory of expansive pedagogy. We conclude with an analysis of the barriers to progress and a call to action, which seeks to provide some solutions to the blocks we have identified.

What is education for?

To what end do we require all our young people to go to school for eleven years or more? There is a cynical view that says school is for minding children while their parents go out to work—and indeed, many adults' lifestyles would have to change radically if there were nowhere for their children to be looked after safely during the day. But if that were the only reason for schools, they could be a lot cheaper and simpler than they are. There would be no need for highly trained teachers, for books and syllabuses, for examinations and qualifications. Children are not just being parked in school; they are not just being kept amused. Societies intend that something beneficial should be happening to them while they are there. Something more worthwhile is meant to be going on. What is it?

There are many different answers to this question, but all of them, implicitly or explicitly, have an image of what the educated 16- or 19-year-old ought to be like. Some say schools are for introducing children to the heritage of the past: to the treasury of Shakespeare's plays, Mendeleev's periodic table, Beethoven's symphonies and Newton's differential calculus. The educated person has knowledge, understanding and an appreciation of the best of their culture. On this view, the syllabus of schools needs to change only slowly, as new cultural products and issues—Harry Potter? Global warming?—acquire this iconic status.

For others, school is essentially a preparation for employment. Once they have mastered the basics of literacy and numeracy, children are on track for a career as a doctor, an engineer, a hairdresser or whatever. To be educated is to be employable. On this view, change is driven by an economic opinion of the national need for different kinds of skilled workers, and by a sense of global competition. It is cheaper to make cars in India or China than in Britain, for example, so car manufacturers will only come to Britain if the levels of skill and productivity in the workforce justify the extra expense.

Perhaps the most widespread view is that schools should somehow achieve an amalgam of these two goals. The aim of education is to develop a mixture of knowledge, understanding and skills to a level that will equip young adults to benefit from further study and training, and to take part in the cultural life of their society. And the aim of educational assessment, crudely, is to sort out those who have achieved these levels, from those who haven't. Some people, mainly politicians, think that tinkering with this model is sufficient. But we don't. We 'expansive educators' think that this 'answer' to the question is too narrow, out-of-date and in many cases damaging to young people's development. And we think that this is partly because it rests on an antiquated and somewhat shallow view of children's minds: how they work, how they grow and what they need.

Education that is truly expansive

Expansive education starts from a different premise. We think that education is, above all, a preparation for the future. Its core purpose is to give all young people the confidence and capacity to flourish in the world they are going to inhabit. We have no idea, for any particular child, what their world will be like. In thirty years' time, today's five-year-olds will be spread across the globe, across occupations, across lifestyles, using technologies neither we nor they can begin to imagine. Beyond the basic literacies of language, mathematics and digital technology, it is hard to say what specific skills or knowledge they are going to need.

So we have to find goals for education that are at a deeper, more generic level. It is a fair bet that, wherever they are, young people will need to be able to make discerning lifestyle choices; to make, maintain and repair friendships; to discover forms of work that are fulfilling and which pose interesting challenges; to enjoy enriching their lives through conversation, reading, art and culture; and to face uncertainties of many kinds with calm intelligence and resourcefulness. We think the development of such capabilities and attitudes has to form the 'core curriculum' of any system of education in the 21st century.

Expansive education is, therefore expansive, in four senses.

First, it seeks to *expand* the goals of education. Traditionally, a school framed its success in terms of its exam results, the quantity and quality of its students' university places, its ratings by independent assessors (such as Ofsted in the United Kingdom*) and by its students' achievements on the sports field and in the concert hall. How students fared after leaving—whether they had genuinely been prepared for the rigours of further study, vocational training and the informal challenges and demands of life—was little monitored and hence little valued. Expansive educators are happy to include these traditional 'success criteria', but insist on adding some more: the extent to which young people's horizons have been broadened so that they have really been prepared to face the tests of life.

Secondly, 'expansive' means *expanding* young people's capacity to deal with these tests. Whereas traditional educators tend to see

---

* Ofsted is the official government body for inspecting schools: http://www.ofsted.gov.uk/

young people's capacity to think and learn as relatively fixed—they talk about students as if they were simply 'bright', 'average' or 'less able'—expansive educators focus on the extent to which our psychological capacities are themselves capable of being stretched and strengthened. What David Perkins calls 'the emerging science of learnable intelligence'[1] has made it clear that a good part of people's so-called intelligence is actually made up of mental habits that can be developed in positive ways. We know that willpower, for example, behaves exactly like a mental muscle that can be strengthened by exercise and depleted through use.[2] Likewise resilience, concentration, imagination and collaboration are all qualities of mind that can be coached and cultivated. This science gives licence to teachers to think of themselves as coaches of the capacities to think and learn. We have explored the many ways in which schools are beginning to draw on an enriched conception of intelligence at some length in our earlier book, *New kinds of Smart*[3], and there is a growing repertoire of well-researched methods which can be used to cultivate thinking and learning.

Thirdly, we are *expanding* our compass beyond the school gates. Expansive education assumes that rich learning opportunities abound in young people's other lives of music, sport and community and family activity. In 1987, Lauren Resnick drew attention to the growing evidence that knowledge acquired outside school can contribute to the development of young people in school—and vice versa. Schooling, Resnick reminds us, is very different from learning outside school.

Briefly, schooling focuses on the individual's performance, whereas out-of-school mental work is often socially shared. Schooling aims to foster unaided thought, whereas mental work outside school usually involves cognitive tools. School cultivates symbolic thinking, whereas mental activity outside school engages directly with objects and situations. Finally, schooling aims to teach general skills and knowledge, whereas situation-specific competencies dominate outside.[4]

To thrive in the real world young people need to experience all eight of the foci suggested in Resnick's list. Anne McCrary Sullivan has compellingly shown through her poetry and scholarly writing, for example, how she acquired the habit of paying attention by following her marine biologist mother on the beach. She explains how her mother, with her buckets, spades and nets, taught her 'attention to the complexities of surface detail and also attention to what lies beneath those surfaces'.[5] Without this expanded palette of learning opportunities, it is unlikely that young people will acquire the kinds of habits of mind which will, for example, not only enable them to use Google when they have access to a computer but also use searching techniques in libraries, supermarkets and town centres when they do not. Expansive educators ensure that their pedagogical and instructional processes reflect this expanded conception of learning.

Fourthly, expansive education has profound implications for the role of teachers. Just as a central clutch of desirable dispositions in young people involve experimenting, noticing, critical thinking, questioning, reflecting and adapting, so the same is true for teachers. Teachers who exhibit these capabilities produce better educational outcomes. John Hattie puts his finger on it most deftly:

The remarkable feature of the evidence is that the biggest effects on student learning occur when teachers become learners of their own teaching, and when students become their own teachers.[6]

In the first half of the sentence, Hattie encapsulates precisely what expansive educators tend to do. They move beyond reflective practice to adopt a more scientific and rigorous mindset with respect to all of their teaching They become better observers of their own effects on students, and more interested in undertaking, publishing and sharing systematic action research with other colleagues. Thus, expansive education requires expansive and enquiring teachers.

This element of ongoing teacher learning is the flipside of the different experiences students have in the classroom when they are undertaking expansive learning. In the web-based community we have created—the Expansive Education Network[7]—teachers undertake their own enquiries in the broad area of expansive education. They are more disposed to adapt and change aspects of their teaching methods to ensure that what they are doing is leading to improvements in student learning, and better at noticing the impacts of their teaching. (See page 51 for more on the Expansive Education Network.)

These four elements of expansive education have major implications for both pupil and teacher experience. Many of the individuals and organisations featured in this book explore the ways in which pupils' learning lives change at school when they live in a world where both traditional subjects *and* their capabilities are valued and where it is assumed that learning is itself learnable.

Cultivating dispositions

Expansive education takes us beyond the realms of knowledge, understanding and even of skills. Resourcefulness, discernment, fortitude and friendship are not mere skills: they are composed of attitudes, values, interests and habitual ways of meeting the world. This difference is crucial and bears exemplifying. The ability to read is a skill. The love of reading is a disposition. As any primary teacher knows, there is a world of difference between a child's being able to read, and being a 'reader'. Thinking skills can be taught, but rarely are these skills brought to bear in real-life situations in which they might be beneficial. Most of us, so the research shows, are able to think much better than we habitually do. The ability to trade opinions over coffee is a social skill. But trustworthiness in relationships is not just a skill; it is a reflection of deeply held values and habits. For their own good, most of us would want our children not just to be able to be honest or kind when it suits them, and not just to espouse the virtues of honesty or kindness, but to behave honestly and kindly because that's the sort of people they are.

Expansive education says:

> *whatever else we are doing in schools, we ought to be consciously, persistently and systematically cultivating the habits and qualities of mind that we think will serve our children well, and which will add to the harmony, prosperity and creativity of the societies they live in.*

Some people might baulk at the use of the word 'ought', but education is irreducibly a moral business. There's no getting away from it: education is a deliberate attempt to create young people who know, think and behave one way rather than another. Schools are teeming with value-laden decisions about what to teach and how. And they also attempt to mould character. They can't not. Do we prefer young people who are acquiescent or sceptical; compliant or critical; committed to 'beating' their peers or inclined to collaborate; eager to give right answers or eager to explore? As a teacher, you can't opt out of these evaluative decisions. You can make them unwittingly and stereotypically, or you can make them knowingly and thoughtfully: that's the only choice you have. Expansive education says it is better to think carefully about the habits of mind you want your students to develop, and then teach accordingly, than to neglect this aspect of your classroom.

Some expansive educators still use the language of skills. They talk about 'life skills', '21st century skills', soft skills' or 'thinking skills'. But we tend to think that 'skills' may not be the best word to capture these qualities of mind. It seems to imply that they can be trained, like the skills of dancing or driving, and many expansive educators don't see the outcomes they are striving for in such a technical fashion. Of course there are techniques that can be learned and taught, which help people to think more clearly or methodically. But expansive educators tend to want to cultivate the attitudes with which young people meet the demands of the world, not just to give them a 'tool-kit' of techniques, which may or may not come to mind when they are needed. As we have pointed out, 'skills' are things that you can do, but not necessarily things that you are inclined or disposed to do. It is no use if, having 'trained' your youngsters in 'thinking skills', those abilities become inert as soon as they leave the classroom (as the research shows they often do). The job of expansive education is to help young people become ready and willing to make use of their abilities.

The Thinking Schools approach (see page 97) is just one example of this shift from skills to dispositional thinking. It aims to develop 'a creative and critical thinking culture [in a school] in which young people learn to understand their own thinking and the thinking of others'. In that context, they offer 'a range of thinking tools and strategies that will become a natural part of a student's repertoire'.[8] The emphasis on the creating of a school culture—not just bolting on a training course in thinking techniques—and on embedding their strategies deeply enough in students' minds so that they become a natural part of the way those students think makes the Thinking Schools approach a truly expansive one.

Because of this dissatisfaction with the word 'skill', many people have coined alternative expressions such as 'habits of mind', 'key competencies', capabilities, attributes, attitudes or learning or thinking 'dispositions'. Others, though, have expressed concern that the language of 'dispositions' or 'attitudes' creates a problem of deciding whether any particular quality is a 'skill' or a 'disposition'. This is an unnecessary worry. A disposition is just a skill that one is disposed to use. In any new situation, one either does or does not have the 'presence of mind'[9] to activate the skill. The issue is not whether 'questioning' is a skill or a disposition. The issue is the degree to which one's tendency to ask questions is robust, widespread and sophisticated. Is your curiosity dependent on being in the company of an encouraging teacher, or is it so strong that you can't not ask questions when they occur to you? Children's 'disposition to be curious', while strong at home, may not yet be robust enough to survive in the face of a busy classroom and, perhaps, a harassed teacher. Does students' questioning attitude show up in many areas of their life—English lessons, science lessons, swimming club and home—or is it confined to just one or two? And are their questions becoming richer and more tailor-made to different situations and subjects? Expansive education sees its job as helping these generic 'skills' to grow into strong, broad and rich dispositions.

The layers of learning

Learning has many layers, and it generally proceeds on several of them simultaneously. Imagine you are taking tennis lessons and playing several times a week. At one level, you are learning by remembering the instructions and explanations you have been told. At another, you are trying to recall and make use of this information as you practise your sliced backhand. You are developing specific skills. But as you play, you are also developing greater physical fitness, strength and flexibility. You are developing a more sophisticated ability to anticipate shots, to read your opponent's game and to think tactically and strategically. In addition, you are learning the etiquette and the 'lingo' of the tennis court and the changing room. By watching and emulating, you are not just learning to play tennis, but to be a 'tennis player'.

So it is in a classroom. Children are learning to remember facts, theories and formulations: the colours of the rainbow, French irregular verbs or the difference between igneous and metamorphic rocks. They are also learning to use this information to enhance their skilled performance—to paint a rainbow, to use the past tense of *avoir* properly, to distinguish between different kinds of minerals—and to talk and write in a way that conveys accurate comprehension. But these are the relative shallows of learning. Below the surface, students are also learning who makes 'knowledge' and who has a right to speculate and create. They are learning the rules of engagement in debate or discussion. They are learning what kinds of learning count as valuable or legitimate (around here) and what gets ignored or disdained. They are learning that mistakes are interesting, informative and inevitable or, alternatively, avoidable signals of ignorance or stupidity. They are learning to think of themselves either as supplicants, able only to remember and understand, or as apprentice critics and evaluators, entitled to interrogate the textbook and ask 'Who says?' and 'How do we know?' They are learning to think of themselves as the masters and explorers of learning, or the dullards and also-rans. Because it is a preparation to live well in uncertain times, expansive education attends to and values these depths of learning as much as the more visible accumulation of knowledge and skill that takes place nearer to the surface.

Who is expansive education for?

The failure to attend to these deeper levels of learning means that schools are not fulfilling their core purpose: to prepare young people to face the challenges of the future with confidence. There are many high-achieving students who struggle at university when the work gets significantly harder, at the same time as the support they get is dramatically less than they were used to receiving at school. The Directors of the Student Counselling Services at both Oxford and Cambridge Universities, for example, are very familiar with such students. Mark Phippen at Cambridge recently told the UK *Times Educational Supplement* (*TES*),

> We are well aware of the number of students who are obviously very academically able but paradoxically lack confidence. That comes about … [largely] because they are being less well prepared [at school] to take on challenges without others helping them out.[10]

Oxford's Alan Percy told the *TES* that today's students:

> often don't grasp the full meaning of learning. Learning is finding out something that you did not know and struggling with it. It's almost as if, if they do not know or understand something immediately, they feel as though they are failing.[11]

Both of them are clear that this situation is getting worse. As the pressure to 'get the grades' increases, so schools inevitably find ways to bite-size and shoehorn students through the tests, often at the expense of their deeper development. No surprise, then, that expansive education—the deliberate cultivation of resilience and resourcefulness—is of great interest to final year colleges and independent schools around the world. It does no justice to expansive education to think of it merely as a kind of compensatory education in life skills for the less able.

However, expansive education is indeed essential for those who are not going to do well in the examination competition. For that is what it is: a competition, in which there have to be losers as well as winners. Despite rhetorical attempts to fudge this uncomfortable issue, some students' good grades only have currency in the marketplaces of university entrance and employment because other students didn't get them. Only 50% of school-leavers in the United Kingdom go on to university. That means half of them don't. For these millions of young people, the also-rans in the grades race, there has to be another way of 'winning' at school—or what was the point? They have to be able to leave school saying, 'I didn't do well on the tests, but I got a really good education—thank you'.

And this has to mean something like: 'You helped me learn how to make friends; how to solve problems; how not to be afraid of difficulty or challenge. You taught me how to think straight, how to talk to all kinds of people and why it is in my own best interests to be kind and honest. You helped me to discover the pride and satisfaction in having struggled to do my best; to value the kinds of intelligence I do have; to believe that the things I was interested in were worth being interested in; to feel that my questions were worth asking. You helped me find my path and my passions, even though they weren't on the syllabus'. Expansive educators believe that putting the deliberate development of these kinds of qualities at the heart of schooling is a matter of basic social justice.

It is a statistical untruth to tell young people that 'everyone can do well if they try'. It's a lie that tries to persuade millions of unscholarly youngsters around the planet every year that the reason they did poorly on the tests was because they lacked 'ability' (they were not intelligent enough) or 'motivation' (they didn't try hard enough). Not only are they disadvantaged in the race for jobs because they didn't do well enough on the tests; they are encouraged to think it is their fault. To expansive educators, this is an iniquity that has to stop. Education is a preparation for life, not just for college or university.

Conventional school success does not make you smart

Good grades don't guarantee a disposition towards good thinking and learning. The number of years of education you have 'consumed' does not predict how well you will argue in the pub, or how you will behave when your plane is cancelled at 11 pm in a country where no-one speaks your language.[12] School teaches you to think about quite specific things, in very specific ways—the ways that will get you a good grade. Being able to churn out short essays or solve well-specified problems under stressful conditions and intense time pressure is not a skill for which there is much call in the world at large.

Real-world learning, thinking and problem-solving are very different. For a start, they are often personally meaningful, ill-defined and collaborative. And we know that skills learned in one context very often do not transfer, even to contexts that look quite similar. The idea that being able to get an A in Latin translations or algebra somehow prepares you to deal well with the complex rough and tumble of everyday life is sadly one that has little empirical support.

Conventional education confuses scholarship with intelligence. Up to a point, it is essential that school helps all young people learn how to read for both information and enjoyment; to write easily and clearly; to express their thoughts verbally and to take part in discussion and debate; to be adept in arithmetic and understand statistics and probability. But not everyone needs to spend their teenage years being trained in the abilities and mindsets of the professor, the lawyer, the actuary or the essayist. Scholarly analysis and argumentation are skills, like other skills. Scholarship is a craft, like other crafts. There is no more reason why every young person should be judged by their ability to think like a professor than to grade them all according to their skill at carpentry.

Being able to argue your case, write a good email and fill in your tax return are useful skills. But so are being able to play the piano, change an ink cartridge, pacify a baby, drive a car, make people laugh, propagate a tray of seedlings and make a curry. And so are being ready to see the world through other people's eyes, question knowledge claims and generate imaginative solutions to problems. Education is getting young people ready to be able to *do* things, especially tricky things, in the real world—not just to analyse them and write about them. People who are primarily makers, movers and do-ers (and whose thinking is in the service of their doing) are just as smart as people who are primarily writers and analysts, and have just as much right to feel that those years in school were well spent.

Differences between expansive approaches

Of course expansive education comes in different varieties. Models of expansive education differ, for example, in the linguistic tone in which they are couched. Some, such as Habits of Mind[13] and Building Learning Power[14], tend to adopt a more vernacular tone, in the hope that young people and their parents will find their approach accessible and appealing. Building Learning Power, for example, speaks informally of teaching in a way that gets students to 'stretch their learning muscles' and makes extensive use of an analogy between developing physical and mental fitness. Habits of Mind talks of 'finding humor' and 'responding with wonderment and awe' as two of its sixteen habits. It includes testimony from students who have benefited from the approach:

> *I can tell you right now that we will never be able to forget the habits of mind. They helped us so much! They taught us better ways of doing things and how to resolve problems!*[15]

Approaches like Habits of Mind and Building Learning Power tend to put a premium on the need to get 'buy-in' from the young people themselves if they are to be successful.

Other approaches adopt a more abstract or scholarly tone, perhaps in the belief that this is necessary if they are to be taken seriously in academic and political circles. The OECD, for example, has written extensively on the need to educate 'competences' (as distinct from 'competencies'), which it defines as 'the ability to successfully meet complex demands in varying contexts through the mobilisation of psychosocial resources'.[16] This might play better in lecture theatres full of policy-makers than in busy staffrooms. It is likely that there are pros and cons either way.

Expansive educators also differ in the particular qualities of mind they single out for development. Some, such as Thinking Schools[17] and Harvard's Visible Thinking[18] program, focus, as their names imply, more on the rational than the social or emotional. They want young people to be ready, willing and able to think critically and carefully, and to understand important ideas deeply. Others foreground the development of more social attitudes. The Flow Foundation[19], for example, is explicitly expansive in its philosophy, when it avers that:

> education systems around the world are failing because of their lack of attention to the development of the fundamental attitudes and abilities that are the very source of personal, social and economic wellbeing.

But the attitudes that it selects to illustrate this concern are 'attentiveness, thoughtfulness, caring, responsibility, tolerance and kindness'. (Interestingly, attentiveness and thoughtfulness are both notions that are simultaneously cognitive and social.) Philosophy for Children[20] spans both camps in its mission to 'encourage children (or adults) to think critically, caringly, creatively and collaboratively'. The

International Baccalaureate[21] Diploma program is built around a 'learner profile', which specifies ten qualities that the program is designed to cultivate. (We explore this further on page 86.)

Recent work by the OECD argues that there is one competence above all which is the over-arching goal of education: adaptability.

Many scholars in the field of education now agree that the ultimate goal of learning and instruction in different subjects consists in acquiring 'adaptive expertise' ... or 'adaptive competence', i.e. the ability to apply meaningfully-learned knowledge and skills flexibly and creatively in different situations. This is opposed to 'routine expertise', i.e. being able to complete typical school tasks quickly and accurately but without understanding.[22]

Broadly, we might say there are three sets of attitudes that expansive educators may want as elements of an empowering 21st century mindset. There are the *communal virtues*, such as honesty, trustworthiness, kindness, tolerance and empathy. There are the *virtues of self-regulation*, which might include patience, self-discipline and the ability to tolerate frustration or disappointment without (as one youngster put it recently) 'kicking off'. (For example, the Habits of Mind approach stresses the importance of building young people's capacity to 'manage impulsivity', and there is a good deal of research—including the famous 'marshmallow test'[23]—to show that the capacity to 'delay gratification' is a powerful predictor of success and happiness in life[24]). And then there are the *epistemic* or *learning virtues*: those that enable one to deal well with challenges and uncertainties, both self-chosen and inflicted. These would include determination, curiosity, creativity and collaboration, for example.

Many different expansive educational approaches have their own list of desirable qualities of mind, and they tend to overlap considerably, while differing in detail and emphasis.[25] Nevertheless, they have much in common. It is unlikely that there will ever be a composite list that suits everyone, and it is probably not a good idea to try to create one. At this stage, it seems healthy that expansive educators can use each other's frameworks to keep their own under review, always capable of being refreshed and enriched.

And with every list, it is not long before the different qualities begin to interweave, and sometimes to conflict. Even the three broad categories of 'virtues' we tentatively identified just now tend to bleed into each other. Patience is a matter of self-regulation, but it is also a vital attitude when faced with a complicated learning challenge. Empathy is a force for good in creating social cohesion (bullies tend to be deficient in empathy), but it is also very useful, in the context of learning, to be able to adopt differing perspectives on an issue. We have already noted that qualities such as 'thoughtfulness' and 'attentiveness' have an inherently dual aspect, embracing both social and cognitive virtues.

The importance of *balancing* these qualities is also recognised by some expansive approaches. (It is explicitly represented as one of the desirable qualities in the IB Learner Profile, for example.) It is generally thought that it is good to be tolerant, and not to meet new people or new ideas with closed-mindedness or prejudice; but it is also good, to many people, to be discerning; to be capable of revulsion or moral outrage when confronted with ideas, actions or images that are repugnant or disgusting. Excess of tolerance becomes moral paralysis; excess of discernment becomes bigotry. Perseverance and determination are good—except when they turn into pig-headedness and intransigence. Sometimes it is good to give up—not because you are feeling stupid and defeated, but because of an intelligent reappraisal of priorities and resources. Creativity and imagination are good—except when what is required is the efficient running of a reliable routine. (It may not be a smart use of time to look for a creative way of brushing your teeth every morning.) Sometimes, the circumspection of 'looking before you leap' is the right choice, and sometimes, the decisiveness of 'fortune favours the brave'. These lists are just the beginning of a conversation; an educative journey that becomes both more seamless and more complex as it unfolds.

Infusion

It should be plain that the expansive philosophy is to find ways of weaving the cultivation of attitudes into the detailed fabric of lessons, as well as every aspect of everyday business in schools. So, when it comes to the relationship between mastering content and cultivating learning dispositions, it is definitely 'both/and' rather than 'either/or'. Useful, transferable habits of mind are being cultivated in the process of—not in competition with—the study of knowledge and the development of skill. You do not have to sacrifice history and mathematics in order to make time for some nebulous, stand-alone activities called 'learning to learn' or 'thinking skills'.

By writing about a historical event through the eyes of different protagonists, you are learning about the workings of the Elizabethan court, say, and you are also stretching your abilities to empathise and imagine. By working in small groups to explore an open-ended challenge involving the calculation of area, you are learning mathematical procedures, and you are also learning to listen respectfully, and to make and test conjectures. Expansive education concerns itself as much with the 'how' of learning as the 'what'. It focuses on the way that young minds are being used and trained day in, day out, lesson after lesson. And it explores ways in which the 'what', the content, can be used imaginatively as a vehicle for developing two kinds of outcomes side-by-side: the ability to understand and manipulate a body of knowledge, *and* the wider dispositions of learning and relating.

So, expansive educators are much more likely to think about cultivating the desired attitudes than merely *teaching* or *training* them. It may help to talk directly with students about the qualities of mind and why they are desirable, and even put on the odd workshop perhaps. But the predominant feeling is that expansive education requires adjusting the way the school works, not simply bolting something new on top. Thus, the booklet that explains the IB Learner Profile invites teachers to ask themselves questions such as:

▶ 'Is it possible to create more experiences and opportunities in the classroom that allow students to be genuine inquirers?'
▶ 'How could we give students more time to develop their ability to work effectively as a team?'
▶ 'Could we create more opportunities to discuss the ethical issues that arise in the subjects we teach?'
▶ 'How well do we model empathy, compassion and respect for others in our classrooms and around the school?'
▶ 'Do our assessment strategies encourage creative and critical thinking?'
▶ 'How well do we report on individual students' development of the qualities in the Learner Profile?'
▶ 'How could we empower students to take more responsibility for their own learning?'[25]

The questions illustrate well the kind of reflective thinking and experimenting that expansive education in general encourages in teachers. As John Hattie said, the attempt to help students develop habits of curiosity and collaboration works much better when teachers themselves are modelling these characteristics in their attitudes to their professional practice, and to each other.

An expansive kind of epistemic apprenticeship

By epistemic, we mean 'to do with the nature of thinking, learning and knowing'. So in this sense, an epistemic apprenticeship is the experience that all young people get of thinking, learning and knowing as they go through their schooling. Of particular importance are the ways in which those dispositions powerfully linked with learning— determination, curiosity, creativity and collaboration—are experienced.

Is the culture of the school one in which determination is encouraged, noticed and celebrated or are teachers quick to step in and answer students' questions? Is asking questions genuinely seen as a good thing or is answering questions the predominant mode of being? Is there a deliberate attempt to cultivate creativity and is this specifically taught in all subjects or is it confined to the creative arts? And is collaboration actively fostered and even assessed or is it viewed with a kind of suspicion leaving teachers uncertain as to 'who has really done the work'? Is it even seen as a form of cheating where 'less able' kids will hang on to the coat-tails of their 'brighter' peers?

Schools that believe in expansive education actively encourage the kinds of habits of mind we have just been exploring. They do this through the language they use, the displays they choose to put on their walls, the notices they post, the reward systems they use and the letters and reports they send to parents. But, more importantly still, they model the kinds of behaviours they purport to value. For it is through the daily exposure to what teachers do and how they behave, rather than what they say they believe, that attitudes and habits are formed. A teacher who talks about how she is struggling to learn something new in her life is a powerful expansive role model. One who shares his own questions, admits to not knowing something but who is resolved to finding out an answer is likely to spawn similar attitudes in his students. It is when teachers genuinely model the expansive habits of mind that we have been exploring in this chapter that expansive education really takes root in a school community. And a powerful way for serving teachers and other educators to demonstrate a willingness to enquire, notice, evaluate, reflect and do things differently and better is through a method such as action research.

We'd like to hope that something that Jason Flom, Director of Learning Platforms at QED Foundation said to us during our research provides a suitable link into the body of our book:

> *A focus on the principles of expansive education—aimed at empowering and enabling students—sends a message that each and every student matters, that they have something valuable to contribute, and that we respect them as learners. It is in this approach to nurturing the mind that we simultaneously nurture their humanity. And by proxy our own.*

Chapter 2

The evolution of expansive education

It is increasingly evident that the educational methods we have been using for the past 70 years no longer suffice. They are based on scientific assumptions about the nature of knowledge, the learning process, and differential aptitudes for learning that have been eclipsed by new discoveries.[1]

Lauren Resnick

We are not the first to use the word 'expansive' in connection with learning. We believe that a Finnish cognitive scientist and adult educator, Yrjö Engeström, initially made this linguistic connection. In the 1980s, he talked of 'learning by expanding'[2], building, for example, on the work of Lev Vygotsky. Then, in 1991, Engeström used the word 'expansive' specifically in connection with learning at school, suggesting that how pupils learn in classrooms should be more like how they find out things in the real world.[3] Specifically, he called for more discovery learning and the creation of classroom contexts in which what is learnt can be practically applied. Engeström has since largely turned his attentions away from school towards the workplace as a place where learning also needs to be made less restrictive.

In the early 1990s, German psychologist Klaus Holzkamp used the term 'expansive learning' to contrast with 'defensive learning'.[4] By the former, he implies that the learner actively chooses to learn to *expand* her options or horizons, while with the latter he is talking about the kinds of learning required in settings such as school, where one can have little choice other than 'going through the motions', because that is what is required.

There are useful elements of what interests us in both Engeström's and Holzkamp's thinking, but we want to go much further. By linking 'expansive' to 'education', we are explicitly choosing to focus on the structures we create to school our young people, and deliberately creating a theory of education which, we believe, is both novel and necessary. In addition, expansive education is also, we will argue, *complex, do-able* (even within regimes focusing largely on narrow measures of attainment) and *worthwhile* (for both learners and teachers).

Expansive Education, as we saw in the last chapter, is about expanding:

1. the goals of school and specifically valued outcomes that go beyond conventional achievement
2. intelligence itself, and the kinds of dispositions that enable young people to be smart and successful throughout life
3. the scope of learning beyond school and university qualifications to include the worlds of home, work, leisure and life
4. the capacity of teachers to be continuous, visible and enthusiastic learners themselves.

Earlier expansive educators

Many educators have espoused aspects of expansive education in the last few centuries. In this quick survey, we try to focus on the lines of thought we can identify in these earlier thinkers that most specifically foreshadow expansive education.

Because of the way early childhood experience sets expectations for the years that follow, a number of influential thinkers have found early education a powerful focus for their ideas. Johann Pestalozzi (1746–1827) tried to bring psychological methods to teaching. He famously remarked that he 'wish[ed] to wrest education from the outworn order of doddering old teaching hacks as well as from the new-fangled order of cheap, artificial teaching tricks'[5] and was concerned to get children to think for themselves. His approach was holistic, combining head, heart and hands, centuries before such approaches became orthodox. In many ways, Pestalozzi was a prototype for today's teachers undertaking action research, endlessly reflecting on the impacts of his experiments.

Friedrich Fröbel, pioneer of the kindergarten system, designed educational play material for preschool children that allowed them to have hands-on involvement in practical learning experiences. Fröbel believed that 'the purpose of education is to encourage and guide man as a conscious, thinking and perceiving being'.[6] He saw play as a way in which children developed their identity within the world and a necessary phase in educating the 'whole' child. He recognised the importance of the child's active role in her own learning.

Rudolf Steiner was a powerful advocate for educating the whole socially developing child, with children being taught in mixed-age, mixed-ability groups. While many educators since have strongly endorsed this whole-child approach, we include Steiner here because of his more fundamentally expansive overall philosophy:

Rudolf Steiner asks us to look at the whole lifespan, to place what happens in childhood in the context of a series of phases that stretches into adult life. His treatment of almost every issue in education is expansive; again and again, he looks at questions from a longitudinal perspective.[7]

Maria Montessori developed an educational philosophy that allowed children to guide their own development within a carefully constructed environment. 'The essential thing is for the task to arouse such an interest that it engages the child's whole personality'[8], she argued. Montessori methods involves mixed-age groups, learner choice of activity, uninterrupted blocks of time within which to work, a constructivist approach to learning whereby learners learn by working with materials rather than through direct instruction and the use of specialised educational materials. Montessori stressed the importance of teachers observing children's development closely, comparing the teacher's role to a naturalist observing bees. The core habit of mind to be developed first was concentration.

Influential cognitive psychologists

A number of well-known psychologists have had a major influence on thinking about learning and learning processes and contributed to our understanding of expansive education today. Jean Piaget, Lev Vygotsky, Jerome Bruner and Reuven Feuerstein are four of the giants on whose shoulders we have stood to develop our version of expansive education.

Jean Piaget's reported definition of intelligence as 'knowing what to do when you do not know what to do' suggests precisely the outcomes any expansive educator might be wanting. Indeed, this definition has become almost a motto for the whole endeavour of expansive schooling. Adaptation—according to Piaget—is the hallmark of intelligent behaviour. Whether, to use his terms, students are *assimilating* new experiences into their world view (fitting practice to theory) or *accommodating* new learning and having to change their ideas to fit with new experiences, they are likely to be expanding their capabilities. For such shifts require perseverance, self-control and the ability to see things from others' perspectives.

> *Intelligence is assimilation to the extent that it incorporates all the given data of experience within its framework ... There can be no doubt either, that mental life is also accommodation to the environment. Assimilation can never be pure because by incorporating new elements into its earlier schemata the intelligence constantly modifies the latter in order to adjust them to new elements.*[9]

Where Piaget's focus was mainly on the development of individual children through interaction with the physical world, Lev Vygotsky was more interested in learning as arising from social activity. He coined the phrase 'the zone of proximal development' to describe the gap between what a learner can do with help and what he or she can do alone. The role of the teacher or more expert peer is to facilitate experiences that are within learners' zone of proximal development, in order to advance their learning. For Vygotsky, the role of the teacher is to 'scaffold' the learner's development of conceptual knowledge by managing the content of learning activities. Vygotsky's contribution to expansive thinking is two-fold. First, he was unambiguous in his belief that children can expand their capabilities with appropriate support from others. Second, he saw the importance of the language of feedback and goal-setting in child development in ways that prefigure what we now think of as formative assessment.

Jerome Bruner saw the purpose of education not as imparting knowledge, but instead as facilitating the development of a child's thinking and problem-solving skills which can then be transferred to a range of situations. Where Piaget spent time seeking to match the level of task to a child's development, Bruner argued that children of any age can cope with most tasks if they are presented appropriately. A proponent (like many in this chapter) of learning through self-discovery, Bruner saw education as expanding the capability to learn. So,

> *Education is not just about conventional school matters like curriculum or standards or testing. What we resolve to do in school only makes sense when considered in the broader context of what the society intends to accomplish through its educational investment in the young. How one conceives of education, we have finally come to recognize, is a function of how one conceives of culture and its aims, professed and otherwise.*[10]

The purpose of education, as he observes, is, of course, intimately tied up with what is going on in the wider world.

Finally, we want to acknowledge the influence of Reuven Feuerstein. Founder and director of the International Institute for the Enhancement of Learning Potential in Jerusalem, Feuerstein's research on what he called 'cognitive modifiability' is part of the evidence base for understanding the value of thinking routines and the idea that the development of these can be fostered. He emphasised the unique propensity of human beings to change or modify the structure of their cognitive functioning to adapt to the changing demands of a life situation.[11]

Arising from his theory of modifiability, Feuerstein developed an approach known as 'dynamic assessment'. Dynamic assessment builds on Vygotsky's idea of the zone of proximal development and invites anyone teaching students to consider what the learner's maximal performance might be, how they can best learn what is required and what teaching is needed to enable them to perform at this level. Habits of Mind creator, Art Costa, cites Feuerstein as the inspiration for at least two of his core dispositions—Striving for Accuracy and Managing Impulsivity.

Progressive expansive educators

In addition to these giants of psychology, there are a number of other important figures in the evolution of expansive education, which we should mention. The philosopher, psychologist, researcher and educational reformer John Dewey prefigured by 50 years much of Bruner's and Feuerstein's thinking. Regularly described as an advocate of progressive education, Dewey wanted a system very different from the one that still predominates today in many parts of the world. Indeed his groundbreaking thinking underpins much (but not all) of what expansive educators today are espousing. Dewey wrote:

> *The teacher is not in the school to impose certain ideas or to form certain habits in the child—but is there as a member of the community to select the influences which shall affect the child and to assist him in properly responding to these. Thus the teacher becomes a partner in the learning process, guiding students to independently discover meaning within the subject area.*[12]

We should note that Dewey's objection to 'habit forming' relies on a narrower view of habits than the one we are taking here. Indeed, John Campbell argues that Dewey could be seen as the founding father of Costa and Kallick's Habits of Mind and other dispositional approaches to education—as this quotation from Campbell makes clear:

> *Further to his argument on reflective thinking, Dewey acknowledges the vital importance of attitudes such as open-mindedness, wholeheartedness and responsibility. He claims that the aim of education is to weave into unity our personal attitudes and our knowledge of the principles of logical reasoning, along with the skills to manipulate these logical thinking processes.*

Dewey's work flows seamlessly into Habits of Mind such as Metacognition, Striving for Accuracy, Thinking Flexibly and Creating, Imagining and Innovating.[13]

Worthy of mention too, as we sketch in the background to expansive education, is Kurt Hahn and his work on the development of what he called Expeditionary Learning. Combining influences from Germany and Britain, Hahn took his ideas to the United States where they are still influential today. His connection with expansive education lies in his belief that learners discover their talents in situations that offer adventure and the unexpected. This led him to see great value in tasks that require the dispositions of perseverance, fitness, craftsmanship, imagination and self-discipline. For Hahn, education often takes place outside school, where risk-taking, collaborative working and respect for the natural world can best be learned.

While Carl Rogers is rightly known as the founder of counselling psychology, it is his emphasis on rethinking the relationship between teacher and learner that connects him usefully with expansive education. When Rogers suggests that 'a person cannot teach another person directly; a person can only facilitate another's learning'[14], he is introducing an approach to teaching which is more about guiding and coaching learning than it is about didacticism. For it is through discovery and exploration that Rogers sees learners developing the dispositions they will need to thrive in life.

Paulo Freire was one of the first explicitly to connect teacher behaviours to the development of certain dispositions in learners. While Freire's political beliefs led him to focus on the development of certain dispositions such as enquiry, respect and democratic participation, his thinking is eminently transferable. And always he is seeking to find authenticity and a sense of what real-world experiences look and feel like.

David Kolb is perhaps best known for his much cited four-stage experiential learning cycle and their associated learning styles.[15]

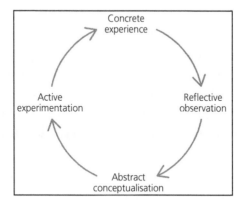

Figure 2.1 Kolb's experiential learning cycle

But while others have (often unhelpfully) become fixated by learning styles, the arguments of Kolb's that interest expansive educators are not so much that any one style could be identified or even measured, but rather that effective learners need to be comfortable in *all* of the modes being suggested by each stage of the learning process. Kolb goes beyond limited notions of intelligence or potential in his thinking and was clearly in this sense making an expansive argument; the dispositions associated with each stage of the learning cycle are not a million miles away from those advocated by many of the expansive pioneers described earlier in this chapter. Of course, learning rarely follows a cycle as predictable as neat diagrams like this suggest!

Our final thinker in this section is Donald Schön. For expansive educators, Schön's major contribution is his insistence that critical, systematic reflection is central to the job of all professionals.[16] Schön refuses to accept the idea that 'scientific' knowledge can only be produced by universities, while schools can only apply (but not create) such knowledge. This powerful line of argument lies at the heart of our belief that teachers, through rigorous enquiry, can contribute to the science and knowledge base as well as effecting application of other people's thinking in their classrooms.[17]

We should note that, of course, there is bound to be disagreement about which movements and thinkers should be included in the pantheon of 'founding fathers' (and mothers) of expansive education. For example, there are some educational approaches that are explicitly called 'character education' that not everyone might want to include within the expansive family. Some such approaches focus strongly on the attempt to inculcate moral values and 'good behaviour', for instance, through the use of a strictly enforced code of behaviour in schools. Some focus on issues of drugs, sexual behaviour or bullying, relying more on frequent exhortations to be a 'good person' (through lectures or posters) than on the more gentle and cumulative attempt to develop the strong habits that we have described above. For many expansive educators, the idea of rigidly enforcing rules of 'politeness'— 'Yes, sir', 'No, ma'am'—does not sit well with their own values. But it is ultimately a matter of personal judgment.

Thinking from the learning sciences today

The thinkers we need to mention in this last section of this chapter are current researchers in exploring aspects of expansive education.

Lauren Resnick is one of the most distinguished psychologists of her generation and the quotation with which we began this chapter suggests one area where she has made an enduring contribution to education—through her focus on learning methods. More specifically, it was Resnick who first initiated a debate about the differences between school learning and learning in the real world in her 1987 Presidential Address to the American Educational Research Association. When, in her speech, she says:

Rather than training people for particular jobs—a task better left
to revised forms of on-the-job training—school should focus its
efforts on preparing people to be good adaptive learners, so that
they can perform effectively when situations are unpredictable
and task demands change[18],

Resnick is echoing the beliefs of expansive educators: that the purpose
of school is to develop the kinds of dispositions young people will
need in order to be able to adapt to whatever life throws at them. In
another seminal article, *Making America smarter*, Resnick offers a
memorable description of intelligence, which exactly presages the
expansive agenda:

Intelligence is working to figure things out, varying strategies until
a workable solution is found. Intelligence is knowing what one
does (and doesn't) know, seeking information and organizing that
information so that it makes sense and can be remembered. In
short, one's intelligence is the sum of one's habits of mind.[19]

Psychologist Martin Seligman has identified the concept of 'learned
helplessness', which exemplifies the problems arising in students who
are not given the opportunity to think of intelligence expansively.[20]
Helplessness of this kind is where students become habituated to
giving up or waiting for someone more knowledgeable to answer any
questions they encounter. They lack resilience and resourcefulness.

On page 54, we give an overview of the work of Harvard's Project
Zero, and its two founders, Howard Gardner and David Perkins,
deserve specific mention. In his book *Frames of mind: the theory of*
multiple intelligences, Gardner famously argued the case for
intelligence being a composite notion:

In the heyday of the psychometric and behaviourist eras, it was generally believed that intelligence was a single entity that was inherited; and that human beings—initially a blank slate—could be trained to learn anything, provided that it was presented in an appropriate way. Nowadays an increasing number of researchers believe precisely the opposite; that there exists a multitude of intelligences, quite independent of each other.[21]

Gardner's theory of 'multiple intelligences' has been widely used (and often misused) to justify the valuing of a range of talents beside those that are purely rational. His approach has been successful in opening up a much broader discussion about intelligence, although he makes no claims for the learnability of each of his eight intelligences.

David Perkins has pioneered expansive thinking in a number of ways. In the 1980s, he focused on one of the most complex aspects of education—learning transfer, or how you ensure that something taught in one context (school, for example) is later available to be used in another situation (at home or at work). In a much-cited paper[22], Perkins and his colleague Gavriel Salomon explored the ways in which, say, spelling skills can be relatively easily transferred from the school classroom where they are learned to a family game at home. This leap is achieved as a result of extensive and varied practice. By contrast, the transfer of an attribute such as 'persistence' from one context to another is an altogether more complex and mindful act, requiring a conscious understanding of the idea as well as practice in many different contexts.

Over the last two decades, Perkins has been hugely influential on this field. His research into what he has termed 'learnable intelligence' sits at the heart of our use of the word 'expansive', proclaiming as it does the fact that intelligence is malleable, not fixed. This insight, he suggests, is as revolutionary in our understanding of human intelligence as was the new thinking about the relation of the sun and

Earth ushered in by Copernicus: 'This revolution in intelligence is ... well-timed for the twenty-first century ... the hopeful new science of learnable intelligence'.[23]

The subtitle of the present book includes the phrase 'for the real world'. And it is in this area that Perkins has also contributed hugely. Building on notions from the work of Yrjö Engeström and Lauren Resnick touched on earlier, Perkins tries to make an explicit connection between what schools do and how learning really happens when students leave formal education. The 'whole game of learning' is Perkins' way of describing a version of learning that is closer to one we might encounter in our adult lives. 'All this sounds very ordinary,' he writes,

> but I'm simply stunned when I think how rarely formal learning gives us a chance to learn the whole game from early on. When I and my buddies studied arithmetic, we had no real idea what the whole game of mathematics was about.[24]

Perkins rejects the possibility that such limited early horizons are simply the inevitable consequence of starting out in any new subject and seeks to show how it is possible to play a game of learning at school which is much more like the game you may end up playing when you leave and how important this is to motivation and engagement. In Chapter 4 we explore how these conclusions can lead to very specific changes in pedagogy.

Robert Sternberg's work on the degree to which intelligence is creative and practical has also influenced our thinking considerably. Sternberg has shown that there are three core aspects of what he calls 'successful intelligence' (what we might equate with real-world intelligence). 'To be successfully intelligent is to think well in three different ways: analytically, creatively and practically.'[25] Yet all too often it is only analytical thinking that is taught and valued in schools.

Sternberg's idea of thinking well can be seen in many of the pioneers that we describe in this chapter.

Carol Dweck has introduced a metaphor of the brain as a muscle, which we find very helpful. In extensive research spanning thirty years, Dweck has shown that, if students think of their brains as like their muscles, capable of being expanded and strengthened through exercise, they try harder, become more resilient and their achievement goes up.[26] Put simply, Dweck is telling us that if you think of your intelligence as expandable, then it is! Unsurprisingly, this evidence sits at the heart of our own thinking about expansive education. Dweck teaches us that we need to focus on the expandability of intelligence, seeking to notice effort wherever we see it if we want students really to thrive. She calls this a 'growth mindset': 'People in a growth mindset don't just seek challenge, they thrive on it. The bigger the challenge, the more they stretch'.[27]

Which are the specific mindsets that help? How can we convert self-belief into actions? What kinds of praise and reward systems work best? Dweck's work raises profound questions about the purpose of schools, their cultures and about the operational details of what goes on between all those working in them. She requires schools to think about almost every aspect of their life from the language they use and the role models they hold up to students to the relationship they have with parents.

In short, individuals who believe that they can become more intelligent through effort do indeed become more intelligent through effort. Many young people across the globe will identify to some degree with Dweck's own early experience:

> *Some of us are trained in this mindset from an early age. Even as a child, I was focused on being smart, but the fixed mindset was really stamped in by Mrs Wilson, my sixth-grade teacher. Unlike Alfred Binet, she believed that people's IQ scores told the whole*

story of who they were. We were seated around the room in IQ order, and only the highest-IQ students could be trusted to carry the flag, clap the erasers, or take a note to the principal. Aside from the daily stomachaches she provoked with her judgmental stance, she was creating a mindset in which everyone in the class had one consuming goal—look smart, don't look dumb. Who cared about or enjoyed learning when our whole being was at stake every time she gave us a test or called on us in class?[28]

Dweck has inspired many of today's thinkers and writers: Geoff Colvin[29], Daniel Coyle[30], Daniel Pink[31] and Matthew Syed[32] are just a few examples. Her influence can be seen in workplaces, in homes, in sports and in schools.

Where Dweck's research stresses the power of mindset, the contribution of Anders Ericsson illuminates the strategies of those who are determined to practise hard. To get really good at something, Ericcson shows us, takes some 10 000 hours of exercise, or what he terms 'deliberate practice'.[33] By the addition of the word 'deliberate', he suggests a degree of single-mindedness and creativity in practising the hard parts, practising in different contexts and so on. The popular writer Malcolm Gladwell has gone on to disseminate many of the ideas of both Ericsson and Dweck in his book *Outliers*.[34]

While Dweck's work has strong implications for the way we talk to students about their work, Ellen Langer is unambiguously interested in the impact of language on creating different cultures. She has shown, for example, how apparently small shifts in language (using 'could be' rather than 'is' when talking about any issue, subject or question) dramatically change a learner's attitudes to what is being discussed.[35] If a complex issue is presented as having a range of plausible explanations, each one of which could be helpful in understanding it, learners are more engaged and keener to contribute their own thinking. But if students are presented with one option that is apparently the only answer, all they can really do is to seek to remember it and file it away in a more passive fashion.

Langer's concept of 'mindfulness' is particularly helpful. She sums it up like this:

> *When we are mindless, we are trapped in rigid mindsets, oblivious to context or perspective. When we are mindful we are actively drawing novel distinctions, rather than relying on distinctions drawn in the past. This makes us sensitive to context and perspective. When we are mindless, our behavior is rule and routine governed. Essentially we freeze our understanding and become oblivious to subtle changes that would have led us to act differently, if only we were aware of them. In contrast, when mindful, our behavior may be guided rather than governed by rules and routines, but we are sensitive to the ways the situation changes.* [36]

The idea of mindfulness places an emphasis on particular kinds of habits and states of mind that we seek to cultivate. So, using 'could be' language invites discussion, multiple perspectives and co-creation, whereas the blunt 'is' invites mindlessness. It gives learners no invitation to be mindful of what is taking place. Expansive classrooms are mindful places where teachers are especially careful to choose vocabulary that invites expansive engagement rather than restrictive learning and mindless passivity.

We cannot end this section without mentioning Sir Ken Robinson. Robinson has an uncanny knack of putting into words what many people feel is wrong with education today, and why it so often ends up feeling restrictive rather than expansive. In his insightful TED talk[37] he describes how formal education arose to meet the needs of industrialism, and that therefore, the most important and highly valued subjects in most schools are those that are useful for work.

Compounding this issue is the way that academic ability has come to be seen as intelligence:

> *If you think of it, the whole system of public education around the world is a protracted process of university entrance. And the consequence is that many highly talented, brilliant, creative people think they're not, because the thing they were good at at school wasn't valued, or was actually stigmatized. And I think we can't afford to go on that way.*

Expansive learning for teachers

If we cannot afford to continue the old ways in the classrooms, the same has to be true of staffrooms. We have to *expand* the ways in which teachers are trained initially and subsequently developed. A number of thinkers have contributed to an expanded conception of professional development that sits side-by-side with our thinking on expansive learning and teaching.

Jean Lave and Etienne Wenger have added a distinctive piece to the expansive jigsaw with their work on 'communities of practice'. Drawing on their anthropological studies of tailors, midwives, supermarket butchers and others, Lave and Wenger help us to understand some important things about groups of people (teachers are of obvious interest to us here) who share a common purpose, work together and seek to learn from their common experiences. According to Etienne Wenger's website, 'communities of practice are groups of people who share a concern or a passion for something they do and learn how to do it better as they interact regularly'.[38]

Lave and Wenger place learning firmly within social relationships. Indeed, they argue that, because all learning is situated in context, it is impossible to understand it according to narrow definitions of skill or knowledge acquisition. As with earlier discussions about learning transfer, context really matters. How one group routinely shares its experiences or organises its time may be very different from how this is undertaken by another, and this impacts on their learning.

School staffrooms are communities of practice and we particularly like the way in which the approach adopted by Lave and Wenger encourages us to think of the apprenticeship undertaken by teachers as they start out and then go deeper in their chosen craft of teaching. Lave and Wenger have coined a specific phrase, 'legitimate peripheral participation', to describe the process by which a newcomer to a community initially watches and learns from the periphery until she or he becomes more attuned to the ways of acting and knowing being demonstrated by the group. Thus, new teachers become socialised by the 'old-timers' into certain semiconscious views and habits as teachers. For expansive educators, it is vital that the community of practice of a staffroom is also a living, evolving community of enquiry.

Chris Watkins has taken Lave and Wenger's ideas, along with many others discussed in this chapter, and blended them together into the idea of classrooms as learning communities. In a move away from the paradigm that says 'learning = being taught', he has focused on the fact that the way a classroom is managed is a more significant variable than any other in terms of helping learning. Taking this as his starting point, he has sought to identify those elements of practice in the classroom community that are most beneficial for learning. Watkins describes a journey from classrooms as *communities* (where the teacher is building a sense of community in which students are actively engaged and have a chance to shape the way things are organised) to those that are *communities of learners* (where the spotlight is on learning rather than on, say, teaching) and finally to classrooms as *learning communities* (in which the emphasis is on the active creation of knowledge by all concerned, including the teacher). The processes attendant on the third of these approaches is, we believe, very likely to lead to a focus on the cultivation of dispositions such as collaboration, enquiry, living with uncertainty, resilience and so on.

Michael Fullan's work also explores cultures of learning especially in schools where the focus is on improving performance. For twenty years, Fullan has argued consistently that teacher enquiry has to be at the centre of the self-renewing school. For him, the presence of enquiry 'indicates that formation and enactment of personal purpose are not static matters but, rather, a perennial quest'.[39] He cites Richard Pascale's helpful assertion that the key disposition in leading change is questioning: 'The essential activity for keeping our paradigm current is persistent questioning. I will use the term *inquiry*'.[40] Fullan has shown how the development of these kinds of expansive learning can also be associated with school improvement. Similarly Ben Levin, sometimes working with Fullan, has shown in his work in Canadian schools how important the creation of a culture of teamwork and enquiry coupled with a focus on teaching and learning is. Levin is interesting in that he combines an academic life with two stints as Deputy Minister of Education for the province of Ontario.[41]

The connection between teachers as learners and school improvement is increasingly being made across the world. Australia's recent *National School Improvement Tool*[42] specifically singles out the importance of schools promoting 'a culture of inquiry and innovation, where creative exploration and independent learning are valued'.

Dylan Wiliam is well known for his championing of formative assessment and, in particular, assessment for learning. But here it is his emphasis on the need for teacher learning communities in which we are interested. Wiliam, like Fullan, wants to change our concept of professional learning. He argues that it is easier for teachers to change their practice when they change their actions and notice the impact of this. Teacher learning communities 'put teachers back in the driver's seat, in charge of their own professional development'.[43]

Far from this being an easy or loose approach, subject to the whims of individual teachers, Wiliam argues for some key components to the conduct of these small communities:

1. Plan to run for at least two years.
2. Start with enthusiastic volunteers.
3. Group teachers with similar assignments.
4. Establish groups with teachers who work together in the same building.
5. Require teachers to make detailed, modest, individual action plans.[44]

Finally, in this group of thinkers who have stressed the importance of teachers as learners is John Hattie. In his magisterial overview of research, *Visible Learning*[45], Hattie makes explicit the connection between teachers undertaking professional enquiry and the benefits that accrue to the quality of student learning and to their attainment, as we showed on pages 6 and 7. Students flourish when their teachers are visible, inquisitive learners themselves, and when teachers continually seek to make visible—explicit and articulate—the students' processes of learning as well.

Hattie's emphasis on 'teachers as learners' as a key mechanism for raising achievement is new and powerful. At a stroke, the two agendas of schooling—getting great results and cultivating dispositions for a lifetime of learning—come together. Teachers, it turns out, need to model their own love of learning and commitment to questioning within a sustained enquiry if their students are to be able to fulfil their potential. To help teachers focus their attentions, Hattie puts into their hands a potent weapon—the research evidence organised in such a way as to be accessible, but not simplistic. Each possible intervention is described and given an effect size, all graphically displayed as a dashboard so that it is clear.

In a more recent book, Hattie is more explicit still about how the role of the teacher needs to change:

> *It is the specific mind frames that teachers have about their role—and most critically a mind frame within which they ask themselves about the effect they are having on student learning. Fundamentally, the most powerful way of thinking about a teacher's role is for teachers to see themselves as evaluators of their effects on students. Teachers need to use evidence-based methods to inform, change, and sustain these.*[46]

For expansive educators, there is growing evidence that precisely the same mindset is required by both teachers and students; one that encompasses the kinds of dispositions for lifelong learning which will enable them confidently to continue learning well throughout their lives.

An example of this can be found in Canada. In a simple experiment, Christina De Simone found that teachers who themselves were initially trained using problem-based approaches were better at incorporating theory and practice into their chosen pedagogy, at defining challenges and at generating solutions in their own teaching.[47] We speculate that their students may similarly be better at problem-solving with such role models. What's sauce for the goose is also sauce for the gander.

These kinds of evidence-based, enquiry-type approaches advocated by Hattie have taken root in various countries across the world. In the United Kingdom, a good example of this is the partnership between the Sutton Trust and the Education Endowment Fund, which has led to the production of a very expansive Teaching and Learning Toolkit.[48] This kind of approach is what David Hargreaves has called a core competence of any self-improving school:

> *The relentless focus on learning and teaching, and the conviction that the best teaching and learning yield high examination and*

test results and rounded persons with the right qualities for a successful life in the 21st century.[49]

Close relatives of expansive education

Hattie's phrase 'visible learning' provides a focus for the last element of our short overview of the foundations of expansive education. We need to link our conception to a number of related notions such as metalearning, metacognition, learning to learn, learning about learning and so forth.

It is a core premise of expansive education that learning to learn is centrally important for all students and teachers. But it must not be seen as an alternative to teaching subject knowledge well and with passion, or as a kind of modular 'add-on', not seen as centrally embedded in all teaching and learning.

That effective strategies for helping students to learn how to learn leads to enhanced performance has been known for some while, and the benefits have been well documented by, for example, researchers at the Institute of Education in London.[50] Interestingly, the Institute has also made explicit the expansive link between inquiry and teachers' practice in the classroom: 'Engaging teachers in critical inquiry fosters a greater alignment between their values and their practices'.[51]

A sophisticated and evidence-based understanding of how to 'do' learning to learn in practice has evolved over the last thirty years. To begin with, the field relied too heavily on a number of simplistic nostrums and 'hints and tips' of dubious scientific validity. For example, some enthusiasts suggested simple causal links between:

▶ high self-esteem and high performance
▶ drinking lots of water and better learning
▶ knowing what multiple intelligences are and, therefore, being better able to select best methods

▶ learning styles and better differentiation of teaching. (Especially un-evidenced here is what is called VAK, an abbreviation for visual, auditory and kineasthetic learning styles which mistakenly confuses temporary learner preferences for particular learning media and methods with unalterable 'styles'. Such an approach can breed helplessness rather than cultivate resilience.)

Guy Claxton has coined the phrase the 'fourth generation'[52] to describe the latest kinds of approaches which, like those discussed in this chapter, are grounded in research. He concludes that: 'Fourth generation approaches to [learning to learn] are interested in fostering this deepening and strengthening of useful learning habits'.[53]

We should also acknowledge the importance of work on metacognition and meta-learning: that is, the values of being able to think and talk about one's own learning and thinking processes. 'Stopping to think' and sometimes 'stopping to think about our own thinking' is self-evidently a very useful disposition to have cultivated.[54] Although, in the spirit of balance, we should note that the capacity to become totally immersed in what you are doing is also highly valuable—and enjoyable. The psychologist Mihaly Csikszentmihalyi has shown that creative and successful learners are able to toggle between total absorption and occasional periods of reflection.

In this chapter, we have highlighted just some of the thinkers on whose shoulders our concept of expansive education sits. We leave the last words in this overview to a contemporary thinker and to a poet–teacher. Researcher Andy Hargreaves sums up well the connection between what society needs and what we are suggesting schools might do:

> *Teaching for the knowledge society, I argue, involves cultivating these capacities in young people—developing deep cognitive learning, creativity, and ingenuity among students; drawing on*

research, working in networks and teams, and pursuing continuous professional learning as teachers; and promoting problem-solving, risk-taking, trust in the collaborative process, ability to cope with change and commitment to continuous improvement as organizations.[56]

And the Nobel prize-winning Indian poet, author and educator Rabindranath Tagore, leaves us with a sense of the profound importance of expansive teaching: 'A teacher can never truly teach unless she is learning herself. A lamp can never light another flame unless it continues to burn its own flame'.[57]

Chapter 3

Current approaches to expansive education

> *What if education were less about acquiring skills and knowledge and more about cultivating the dispositions and habits of mind that students will need for a lifetime of learning, problem-solving and decision-making? What if education were less concerned with the end-of-year exam and more concerned with who students become as a result of their schooling? What if we viewed smartness as a goal that students can work toward rather than as something they either have or don't?*[1]
>
> *Ron Ritchhart*

What indeed!

In this chapter we look across the world at the work of some of those currently pioneering the new generation of approaches to expansive education. We have obviously not been able to include every organisation offering expansive approaches to education. Rather, we have selected a representative sample from which we hope other expansive educators can learn. We will continue to document further exemplars on our website[2] and we hope reading this book will encourage you, and other expansive initiatives you know, to make contact with us.

As we assemble more and more examples of expansive education practice, we are trying to find out exactly how people are thinking about what they do, what outcomes they are noticing, what theories are driving their thinking and where it is working best at the school level. We are constantly trying to learn about how we can best prepare young people for a lifetime of uncertainty, while at the same time ensuring that they do as well as they can in whatever public examination system they find themselves in. In this chapter, we will be giving examples of expansive practice at each of four levels: international, national, regional and very local (often at the individual school level). And, given our four facets of expansive education, we are also going to be tracing pioneering activity in:

1. expanding the goals of education to include expansive dispositions
2. demonstrating the learnability of intelligence in a variety of ways
3. looking at the benefits of expansive education for life beyond school, college and educational qualifications
4. developing the culture and practices of enquiring teachers.

This chapter is organised loosely around these four dimensions of expansive education and groups stories and case studies according to which dimension they most fit with. Within each section we have deliberately mixed up local, regional, national and international organisations and initiatives. Inevitably, the four categories are permeable and some examples could have easily been linked to a different 'dimension' or, indeed, to more than one. Some approaches, like that of Ron Ritchhart and colleagues at Harvard's Project Zero[3], have explored several aspects of expansive education. Others have gone deep into one area. Some organisations and approaches, like Habits of Mind and Building Learning Power, are in use across the world. Others exist at the national level, such as the Singapore or New Zealand National Curricula. Many operate regionally or locally.

Several examples span both research and practice as in the case of Project Zero or of our own small Centre for Real-World Learning at the University of Winchester.[4] Some approaches are deeply grounded in research, such as Carol Dweck's Mindset Works, while others have grown from grassroots practice. Some are commercial, while others are not-for-profit organisations. We have found expansive publishers, trainers, campaigning bodies, groups of schools and awarding bodies. Thousands, probably tens of thousands, of individual schools are choosing to adopt educational approaches that are clearly expansive and we have included just a few individual school examples.

As we looked across the world our spirits soared. For, despite an incredible fragmentation (and in some places confusion) of educational practices and rhetorics, there is something that looks suspiciously like a movement growing (albeit organically) out there. Noticeable, too, was the passion with which these educators talked of their endeavours. Busy founders, heads and chief executives of expansive organisations were keen to engage in conversation about what it is they do that ultimately makes a difference to the lives of children and young people on a day-to-day basis. A growing band of educators—the increasingly restrictive and narrowly performance-driven nature of some educational systems notwithstanding—believe that the moral purpose of education *has* to be expansive and that there is *good* evidence from the learning sciences and from educational research that young people achieve more when they are taught expansively.

Our own journey

For several decades we have been exploring aspects of expansive education ourselves. 'Learning through Landscapes', 'Building Learning Power', 'learning to learn', 'family learning and parental engagement', 'dispositions for learning', 'pupils as teachers', 'thinking skills' and 'learnable intelligence' are just some of the areas in which we have personally invested time and energy. Of our list of key words, 'learnable intelligence', the phrase coined by David Perkins[5], has assumed a central importance for us. For, beliefs around the fixity of intelligence are not only scientifically weak but also morally repugnant when it comes to designing an education system that is of genuine benefit for all young people.

Our thinking has been sharpening in other ways too. For example, just because activities take place outdoors or in the community does not necessarily make their intentions expansive. Creating and planting a garden may not make a child more resourceful or collaborative. It depends on *how* it is done. Approaches such as Building Learning Power do not work if they are simply bolted on to an otherwise restrictive approach. Learning to learn cannot be confined to modules or discrete sessions. It needs to be accompanied by a more pervasive commitment to empowering learners with a rich and relevant language for learning. Schools that really engage parents, we have come to see, have to rethink the implicit psychological contract they have with them.

Above all, we have come to believe that we have to find a way of achieving both conventional success (as typically measured by public examinations) *and* success in dealing with the uncertainties of the real world. We need an 'and' approach, not the traditional 'or'. We want to have our cake and eat it. We recently found help in articulating this wish from a surprising source. *First steps: a new approach for our schools* is a report from the Confederation of British Industry (CBI), the major British employers' organisation. Its first recommendation is:

> *[The] development of a clear, widely-owned and stable statement of the outcome that all schools are asked to deliver. This should go beyond the merely academic, into the behaviours and attitudes*

schools should foster in everything they do. It should be the basis on which we judge all new policy ideas, schools and the structures we set up to monitor them.[6]

A number of countries across the world are trying to go for the 'and' not 'or' model. Singapore is a case in point and we return to this example later in this chapter. In Chapter 4, we lay out some of the choices that all teachers are required to make daily, weekly, termly and yearly as they seek to ensure that young people are not the victims of such 'or' thinking.

The Expansive Education Network

Over the past two decades, we have had the privilege of working with many wonderful researchers, school leaders, business people, social entrepreneurs, policy-makers, parents, students and classroom teachers. But although we have found some extraordinary pioneers, we have not found any one person or organisation who is systematically exploring *all four* of our expansive dimensions. That's why we have created the Expansive Education Network[7], (eedNET, for short), to bring pioneering educators together in a global learning community. Before we offer snapshots and stories from across the world, we focus on eedNET as an example, to set the scene.

Example: Expansive Education Network

eedNET is a kind of professional learning community. It brings together teachers, researchers and providers of all kinds to find out more about expansive education. In the main it is a creative commons on which any expansive educator can 'graze'. A network of universities and partner organisations teach teachers how to undertake their own professional enquiries using the methods associated with action research. In three after-school workshops, we equip teachers with the necessary habits of mind, skills and understanding to undertake their own research, publish it on eedNET and then share it widely with their colleagues.

We ask potential participants whether they agree or disagree with five (deliberately loaded) interlinked statements:

1. It is essential that 21st century education focuses on developing young people's aptitude and appetite for learning, in school and out.
2. *All* young people, in all kinds of schools and colleges, can be helped to become more confident and capable learners.
3. Developing openness, inquisitiveness, resilience and imagination is as important for high-achievers as it is for low.
4. This aim also helps students do better on tests—there is no necessary conflict between raising standards and developing learning aptitude.
5. We already know a good deal about how to do this, but there is a lot more to find out.

If they can agree with all of these, they tend to choose to join eedNET. At the very least, they are likely to be sympathetic to the premises of expansive education and may be intrigued enough to browse more.

By way of 'nourishment' on the site, each month we feature:

- a school making real attempts to embed expansive education
- one or more useful publications
- a piece of published research which adds to our understanding
- an example of a report produced by a teacher undertaking action research in his or her school.

On a termly basis, we produce a teacher-friendly digest of research and practice on an aspect of expansive education. Examples already published include 'Teaching for transfer' and 'Learners becoming teachers'.

At the heart of eedNET is a three-way dialogue between teachers, sympathetic universities and pioneering advocates of expansive education. Initially, we assembled a group of ten universities in the United Kingdom. But almost immediately we welcomed another from Australia[†] and by the time you

---

† Deakin University

read this the only way of finding out who our current partners are will be to go to www.expansiveeducation.net and check for yourself!

At the same time, we have identified a number of organisations that deliver some aspect of expansive education and have begun to work with them. Our early list has a mainly (but not exclusively) United Kingdom flavour and includes:

- ASDAN Education
- Building Learning Power
- Centre for the Use of Research and Evidence in Education (CUREE)
- Eden Project
- Institute for Habits of Mind (USA)
- Philosophy for Children
- RSA Opening Minds
- Expansive Learning Network.

Later in this chapter we tell the story of each of these initiatives, as well as of many other organisations.

For many teachers and educators the Expansive Education Network is a free resource. But for a growing number it is a source of professional learning. Each university partner delivers three sessions to teachers on the art and craft of action research (sometimes called teacher enquiry). The model we have evolved here is deliberate. All sessions are 'twilight'—that is to say occurring outside the formal school teaching day—and therefore more easily and cheaply accessible to teachers. These sessions are deliberately practical, empowering teachers to get enough skill and confidence in action research to get going on an enquiry of their own. The final session is celebratory, with teachers presenting their findings and sharing their further ideas for enquiry with other colleagues. Teachers produce posters, learning mats, film clips and reports, and we host a library of these in the members-only area of the site. In the future we aspire to making all resources freely available. In this vein, each pioneer and all university partners commit to providing some resources freely for the good of the wider community.

A not-for-profit funder—the Comino Foundation—and a global education business—Pearson—provided us with start-up funds without which the venture could not have been born.

Stories from the frontline of expansive education: developing expansive dispositions

Example: Project Zero, Visible Thinking and Studio Thinking

One of the most influential forerunners of expansive education is Project Zero, a research and development project founded at Harvard University in 1967 by the eminent philosopher Nelson Goodman. As we said in Chapter 2, Project Zero's founding directors were Howard Gardner, whose work on multiple intelligence it spawned, and David Perkins, whose research laid the foundations for the now widespread interest in the science of learnable intelligence. Originally focused on developing learning in the arts, Project Zero has expanded and diversified over the years to create a suite of different projects that deal with all subjects and all levels within education.

One of these was the Making Learning Visible project, initially directed by Gardner and art educator Steve Seidel, who took over the direction of Project Zero as a whole from Gardner and Perkins in 2000. The project explored the value of learning groups documenting their own learning processes. More recently, Ron Ritchhart and colleagues have developed this work into a project on Visible Thinking, which aims to make the teaching of thinking dispositions an explicit goal across the whole age range of students in education. They focused on the development of six dispositions which they consider key: careful observing and describing; building explanations and interpretations; reasoning with evidence; making connections; considering different viewpoints and perspectives; and forming conclusions. (See the case study of Bialik College below.)

Another more recent project on Studio Thinking has stayed closer to Project Zero's roots in arts education. Led by Lois Hetland and Ellen Winner, Studio Thinking has carefully distilled out the ways in which learning in the context of arts and crafts can develop positive dispositions towards learning in general. Their list of dispositions includes developing the habits and mindset of a craftsman, learning careful and patient observation, persisting with difficulty, dealing with frustration and imagining and envisioning processes and outcomes. Key aspects of the studio environment which helped to foster the development of these dispositions included short, stimulating presentations and demonstrations to fire students' imaginations, plenty of time spent working on projects independently to build persistence and resilience and regular peer-review sessions in which students can cultivate the dispositions of reflecting and giving and taking feedback.

Overall, Project Zero, and the many sub-projects to which it has given rise over the years, has had a massive impact on the development of expansive education around the world.

• •

A school example closely aligned to Project Zero is Bialik College in Melbourne, Australia.

School case study: Bialik College

Bialik College is an independent, coeducational Jewish school in a suburb of Melbourne, Australia, that caters for around 1000 students, of many nationalities, from kindergarten through to upper secondary level. Since 2006, Bialik has been collaborating with the Visible Thinking team at Harvard's Project Zero on a school-based project called 'cultures of thinking'. This project has formed one of the major foundations for a book called *Making Thinking Visible*, by Ron Ritchhart, Mark Church and Karin Morrison, published in 2011.[8] Karin was Deputy Principal at Bialik and led the in-school team for the first five years of the project.

The project explores the process of embedding the use of 'thinking routines' into everyday lessons and activities, with the objective of building strong dispositions in students towards good, careful creative thinking. The routines are focused enough to get students to use their minds in specific ways, yet broad enough to be applicable to a wide range of subject matter. One of the routines is called See–Think–Wonder, or STW for short. Students might be given an image or a diagram, or shown a piece of video, and asked first to concentrate on the actual detail of what has been presented. They might be asked to write or talk very objectively about what they see, trying to be both neutral and meticulous in their observations. Then, as a second stage, they are asked to develop possible interpretations—to ask themselves (or each other) 'What might be going on here?' Students might be required to link their observations with their inferences by being asked, 'What do you see that makes you think that?' By being questioned again and again in this way, the intention is to build habits of mind that distinguish between facts and opinions, and which respect the evidence that lies behind people's knowledge claims. In a final stage, students are encouraged to wonder and speculate aloud about wider issues and questions that might be raised by their more disciplined thinking.

For example, Caitlin Faiman was teaching a Grade 5 maths class, and she wanted the students to appreciate that maths was not just something they did in school, but was all around them. So she showed the students MC Escher's drawing 'Night and Day', in which patterns gradually turn into white birds on the 'night' side of the picture and black birds on the 'day' side. First, she revealed just a single unambiguous bird, and then, gradually, more and more of the whole image, getting the students to see how their 'See–Think–Wonderings' changed as their information expanded. As students appreciated more and more of the geometric properties of the image, so their mathematical conversations became very rich. Caitlin observed: 'Students saw so much maths! Our conversation touched on symmetry, transformation, direction, triangular numbers, congruency, reflection and 2D and 3D shapes.'

• •

Another widely used and influential example of expansive education is Habits of Mind.

Example: Habits of Mind

In the 1980s, Art Costa, then Professor of Education at California State University at Sacramento, set out to discover what it is that intelligent people do when they are confronted with problems, the resolutions of which are not immediately apparent. Having scoured the literature and asked a dozen eminent thinkers in the area, he formulated a list of the most important 'habits of mind' that seemed to characterise such people. The Habits of Mind approach derived support from the work of a number of thinkers including John Dewey, Arthur Whimbey and Robert Sternberg. Over the succeeding years, largely in collaboration with educator Dr Bena Kallick, Costa has refined his list of habits into 16:

1. Persisting
2. Thinking and communicating with clarity and precision
3. Managing impulsivity
4. Gathering data through all senses
5. Listening with understanding and empathy
6. Creating, imagining, innovating
7. Thinking flexibly
8. Responding with wonderment and awe
9. Thinking about thinking (metacognition)
10. Taking responsible risks
11. Striving for accuracy
12. Finding humor
13. Questioning and posing problems
14. Thinking interdependently
15. Applying past knowledge to new situations
16. Remaining open to continuous learning.

Having now worked with thousands of schools, Costa and Kallick have developed a wide range of effective classroom practices for engaging and developing each of these intelligent habits.

Their basic vision is that schools should prepare young people 'not just for a life of tests, but for the tests of life'. In the introduction to one of Costa and Kallick's best known books *Discovering and Exploring Habits of Mind*[9], Harvard Professor David Perkins put it this way:

> This book speaks not just to intelligence in the laboratory but also to intelligent behaviour in the real world. It addresses how we can help youngsters get ready for the road of life, a sort of 'drivers' education' for the mind ... When today's students hit the road, the ideas in Habits of Mind can help them ride on smooth mental wheels.

Costa and Kallick have also pioneered ways of tracking and recording the development of these habits, and have thus been able to amass a good deal of evidence for the effectiveness of this approach. For example, teachers can use a variety of observation schedules to check how robustly and how frequently particular habits of mind are being used in their classes. Even in terms of school achievement, it turns out that the best-performing students possess and deploy a broader range of habits of mind, more effectively and appropriately, than do lower-achieving students.[10] Costa and Kallick argue that assessing the growth of habits of mind is best done in collaboration with students, so that, through their involvement, they naturally come to be better at self-assessing and self-regulating.

The Institute for Habits of Mind[11] acts as a focus for the work and a community of practice. Habits of Mind has taken root across the world with very active communities in Australia, New Zealand, North America and the United Kingdom.

Habits of Mind is a founding pioneer member of the Expansive Education Network.

• •

The influence of Habits of Mind can be seen across the world. Here we offer one example from a school in Hawaii.

School case study: Waikiki School

Waikiki School serves nearly 400 students from kindergarten through to Grade six. 40% of the students qualify for free or reduced-cost school meals, 26% require additional 'English Language Learner' (ELL) assistance, 8.4% require special education services and 40% live in single-parent homes. Despite the intensity of its student needs, Waikiki continues to exceed all national and state standards and has been recognised as a Hawaii Distinguished School each year since the inception of this award. Its unique curriculum couples instruction in the Hawaii State Content Standards with instruction in the Habits of Mind approach. The infusion of this model within standards-based instruction defines the strength of Waikiki School—what the school refers to as its 'mindfulness' approach.

Waikiki Elementary School's evolution to a 'Mindful School' began in 1991. Mindfulness was not adopted at the Waikiki School to promote a good feeling. On the contrary, it was brought in to help students with their thinking skills in order to raise scores on statewide testing, and to improve academic results school-wide. The school believes that the best way to develop students' thinking skills is to use them every day, and to think about thinking every day.

Initially, a series of workshops for staff and parents was conducted and as a result of these the staff adopted Habits of Mind, which over the past 17 years have been integrated into the curriculum and have become the expected norm throughout the school. Over the years, other staff development experiences have extended and enriched the staff's understanding of curriculum integration, authentic assessment, direct teaching of thinking skills, concept development, cognitive coaching, Philosophy for Children, collaborative learning and thematic unit planning.

At Waikiki School, Habits of Mind are prominently displayed in the office, on bulletin boards, in the cafeteria, on the ceiling of the main walkway and in every classroom. Children learn age-appropriate definitions and applications for these behaviours, beginning in kindergarten. In the playground, they are used as a reference for analysing choices, especially in situations requiring discipline. Habits of Mind are also integrated into daily classroom assignments and discussions; they are an active vocabulary of the Mindful School culture.

The program at Waikiki has a language of its own. There are 'magic words' which serve the purpose of class management. 'POPAAT' can be mentioned by any student to remind everyone, 'Please, one person at a time'. 'PSL' stands for 'please speak louder' which students say when they can't hear their classmates. The magic words empower students to help keep the conversation on topic and within accepted boundaries. There is also a toolkit to help students with their thinking. 'Assume', 'inference', 'true', 'reason', 'example', 'counter-example' and 'What do you mean by that?' are all words in the toolkit.

In addition to the tests they take at school, Waikiki School students are prepared to perform well on the 'tests of life'. Teachers and staff don't simply teach values; rather they seek to model the behaviours they want to see developed. Teachers are encouraged to be individuals in the classroom and exercise their strengths and creativity. In a sense, the whole school is on the same page, but every page is wonderfully different.

••

Wider frameworks for personal learning and thinking skills

During the late 1990s in England, the government department with responsibility for education (then called the Department for Children, Schools and Families) actively supported the development by one its executive bodies, the Qualifications and Curriculum Agency, of a framework that sought to bring together the kinds of dispositions and wider skills to which all educated students should aspire. This became

Table 3.1 A framework for Personal, Learning and Thinking Skills[12]

	Focus	Young people
Independent enquirers	Young people process and evaluate information in their investigations, planning what to do and how to go about it. They take informed and well-reasoned decisions, recognising that others have different beliefs and attitudes.	● identify questions to answer and problems to resolve ● plan and carry out research, appreciating the consequences of decisions ● explore issues, events or problems from different perspectives ● analyse and evaluate information, judging its relevance and value ● consider the influence of circumstances, beliefs and feelings on decisions and events ● support conclusions, using reasoned arguments and evidence.
Creative thinkers	Young people think creatively by generating and exploring ideas, making original connections. They try different ways to tackle a problem, working with others to find imaginative, valuable solutions and outcomes.	● generate ideas and explore possibilities ● ask questions to extend their thinking ● connect their own and others' ideas and experiences in inventive ways ● question their own and others' assumptions ● try out alternatives or new solutions and follow ideas through ● adapt ideas as circumstances change.
Reflective learners	Young people evaluate their strengths and limitations, setting themselves realistic goals with criteria for success. They monitor their own performance and progress, inviting feedback from others and making changes to further their learning.	● assess themselves and others, identifying opportunities and achievements ● set goals with success criteria for their development and work ● review progress, acting on the outcomes ● invite feedback and deal positively with praise, setbacks and criticism ● evaluate experiences and learning to inform future progress ● communicate their learning in relevant ways for different audiences.

	Focus	Young people
Team workers	Young people work confidently with others, adapting to different contexts and taking responsibility for their own part. They listen to and take account of different views. They form collaborative relationships, resolving issues to reach agreed outcomes.	● collaborate with others to work towards common goals ● reach agreements, managing discussions to achieve results ● adapt behaviour to suit different roles and situations, including leadership roles ● show fairness and consideration to others ● take responsibility, showing confidence in themselves and their contribution ● provide constructive support and feedback to others.
Self-managers	Young people organise themselves, showing personal responsibility, initiative, creativity and enterprise with a commitment to learning and self-improvement. They actively embrace change, responding positively to new priorities, coping with challenges and looking for opportunities.	● seek out challenges or new responsibilities and show flexibility when priorities change ● work towards goals, showing initiative, commitment and perseverance ● organise time and resources, prioritising actions ● anticipate, take and manage risks ● deal with competing pressures, including personal and work-related demands ● respond positively to change, seeking advice and support when needed ● manage their emotions, and build and maintain relationships.
Effective participators	Young people actively engage with issues that affect them and those around them. They play a full part in the life of their school, college, workplace or wider community by taking responsible action to bring improvements for others as well as themselves.	● discuss issues of concern, seeking resolution where needed ● present a persuasive case for action ● propose practical ways forward, breaking these down into manageable steps ● identify improvements that benefit others as well as themselves ● try to influence others, negotiating and balancing diverse views to reach workable solutions ● act as an advocate for views and beliefs that may differ from their own.

known as Personal, Learning and Thinking Skills (PLTS) and similar approaches were adopted in Scotland and Northern Ireland.

PLTS creator, Mick Waters, is a strong supporter of the Expansive Education Network today. Waters has gone on to create The Curriculum Foundation[13] in the United Kingdom, in a deliberate attempt to support schools that want to take a more expansive approach to curriculum development by developing broader competencies such as critical thinking, problem-solving, communication, creativity, cooperation and independent learning. The PLTS provided a level of support for teachers in England wishing to teach in more expansive ways. But we have not included them as a national education ministry example in this chapter for the simple reason that the rest of the English National Curriculum at this time took a different (sometimes, irreconcilably) and far less expansive approach.

A similarly broad view of the goals of education has been taken by one advocacy group in the USA.

Example: Partnership for 21st Century Skills

In the United States, the Partnership for 21st Century Skills (P21) has, since 2002, advocated for a greater emphasis on wider skills in American schools. The organisation acts as a catalyst to promote debate and encourage new thinking around this core premise. It calls for 3Rs (though not the traditional ones) and 4Cs:

▶ The 3Rs include: English, reading or language arts; mathematics; science; foreign languages; civics; government; economics; arts; history and geography.
▶ The 4Cs include: critical thinking and problem solving; communication; collaboration; and creativity and innovation.

As the 3Rs serve as an umbrella for subjects and core content, the 4Cs are shorthand for all the skills needed for success in college, career and life.[14]

P21 is an example of a group operating at scale in a large and diverse nation such as the United States, where it is seeking policy changes to make education more broadly expansive. In the United Kingdom, the Twenty-First Century Learning Alliance performs a similar intelligent advocacy function.

• •

Some organisations have chosen to focus on certain thinking skills seen to be underdeveloped.

Example: Mind Lab

A commercial approach to developing dispositions can be seen in the work of Mind Lab. The Mind Lab approach was developed by two chess masters, Ehud Shachar and Dan Gendelman, in Israel in 1994, in response to their growing frustration at a lack of resilience and staying power in the children they were teaching to play chess. It is a games-based approach to the development of such skills as decision-making, memory training, sequencing, social cooperation, research methods and spatial thinking. Mind Lab UK was a founding pioneer organisation supporting the Expansive Education Network.

• •

Competence-based approaches

For many years, educators have been wrestling with the tension between the way schools are organised around subjects and the fact that in the real world, and even in really absorbing learning in schools, traditional subject boundaries may not be the best way of chunking up the curriculum. An alternative view, which has found favour in some parts of the world, is competence-based education. This approach has long been associated with vocational education where the goal is more obviously concerned with the practical outcomes of teaching. For example, it is clear that we would want a surgeon to be able to understand human systems and have considerable manual dexterity with a scalpel, just as we would expect a plumber to understand the workings of a complex heat-exchange boiler and be able to diagnose a non-routine fault.

Example: The European Key Competences for Lifelong Learning

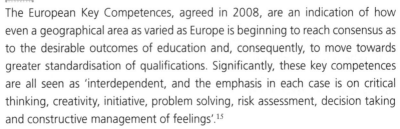

The European Key Competences, agreed in 2008, are an indication of how even a geographical area as varied as Europe is beginning to reach consensus as to the desirable outcomes of education and, consequently, to move towards greater standardisation of qualifications. Significantly, these key competences are all seen as 'interdependent, and the emphasis in each case is on critical thinking, creativity, initiative, problem solving, risk assessment, decision taking and constructive management of feelings'.[15]

The eight key competences are:

▸ **communication in the mother tongue**, which is the ability to express and interpret concepts, thoughts, feelings, facts and opinions in both oral and written form (listening, speaking, reading and writing) and to interact linguistically in an appropriate and creative way in a full range of societal and cultural contexts

▸ **communication in foreign languages**, which involves, in addition to the main skill dimensions of communication in the mother tongue, mediation and intercultural understanding. The level of proficiency depends on several factors and the capacity for listening, speaking, reading and writing

▸ **mathematical competence and basic competences in science and technology**, which is the ability to develop and apply mathematical thinking in order to solve a range of problems in everyday situations, with the emphasis being placed on process, activity and knowledge. Basic competences in science and technology refer to the mastery, use and application of knowledge and methodologies that explain the natural world. These involve an understanding of the changes caused by human activity and the responsibility of each individual as a citizen

▸ **digital competence**, which involves the confident and critical use of information society technology (IST) and, thus, basic skills in information and communication technology (ICT)

- **learning to learn, which is related to learning**, the ability to pursue and organise one's own learning (either individually or in groups, in accordance with one's own needs) and awareness of methods and opportunities
- **social and civic competences**, which refers to personal, interpersonal and intercultural competence and all forms of behaviour that equip individuals to participate in an effective and constructive way in social and working life. It is linked to personal and social wellbeing. An understanding of codes of conduct and customs in the different environments in which individuals operate is essential. Civic competence, and particularly knowledge of social and political concepts and structures (democracy, justice, equality, citizenship and civil rights), equips individuals to engage in active and democratic participation
- **sense of initiative and entrepreneurship**, which is the ability to turn ideas into action. It involves creativity, innovation and risk-taking, as well as the ability to plan and manage projects in order to achieve objectives. Individuals are aware of the context of their work and are able to seize opportunities that arise. It is the foundation for acquiring more specific skills and knowledge needed by those establishing or contributing to social or commercial activity. This should include awareness of ethical values and promote good governance
- **cultural awareness and expression**, which involves appreciation of the importance of the creative expression of ideas, experiences and emotions in a range of media (music, performing arts, literature and the visual arts).

To enable these competences to be measured across the countries of Europe, the European Key Qualifications Framework[16] has been created. This is an example of a significant number of countries being asked to ensure that all of their qualifications can be mapped against a common framework, in order to describe the consistency and transferability of competences being developed across a large economic area.

• •

Some of the competences listed above definitely fit within the scope of the expansive dispositions we are seeking to cultivate in young people. 'Learning to learn' and a 'sense of initiative and entrepreneurship' obviously fit into this category. Most are ways of describing progress within subjects in ways that move away from 'knowledge' towards broader skills, although some have aspects of expansiveness within them.

Of course, whether a competence-based approach is expansive depends on which competences are selected (whether these are largely instrumental or job-related or to do with becoming a more powerful learner). There is also a legitimate debate about the degree to which competences can be considered without reference to the context in which they are being developed. If they are too generic they may have little meaning for students, but if too specific, they may not be meaningful in a range of different situations.[17]

A few examples from national (or large state) education ministries may be of interest here.

Ministry of Education case study: Romania

In Europe, the Romanian National Curriculum is an example of one that has been heavily influenced by a competence-based approach. But an analysis of its curriculum for mathematics indicates the expansive imagination that has been at work in its creation. So high school students are required to:

- demonstrate curiosity and imagination in creating and solving problems
- manifest tenacity, perseverance and the capacity of focusing on problems
- manifest a spirit of objectivity and impartiality
- develop independence in thought and action
- demonstrate initiative and interest in approaching various tasks
- manifest confidence in using technology
- develop, in an aesthetic and critical sense, an appreciation of rigour, order and elegance in the architecture of problem solving or theory building
- develop the habit of making use of mathematical concepts and methods in approaching everyday situations or in solving practical matters
- develop motivation for studying mathematics, as a relevant field for social and professional life.[18]

These are an eclectic and interesting set of attributes or habits of mind to be explicitly linked to and embedded in the study of mathematics.

••

For several decades, Australian states have pioneered thinking in these kinds of areas, too.

Ministry of Education case studies: Australia

South Australia
In 1999, South Australia began its Learning to Learn project, which sought to change the way that teaching and learning was conceptualised in that state. One very useful resource from the first decade of the project's development work is the South Australian Teaching for Effective Learning Compass[19], which provides a kind of map for teachers to consider ways in which they can make their own teaching more broadly expansive.

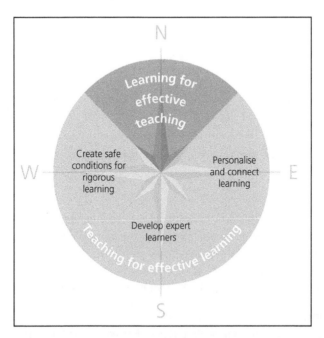

Figure 3.1 South Australian Effective Learning Compass

The Compass has two elements, Learning for Teaching and Teaching for Learning.

Learning for Teaching is divided into a number of areas:

▶ understanding how self and others learn
▶ developing deep pedagogical and content knowledge
▶ participating in professional learning communities and networks
▶ engaging with the community
▶ discussing educational purpose and policy
▶ planning and organising for teaching.

Teaching for Learning has three sub-sections.

Table 3.2 Teaching for learning

Teaching for learning		
Create safe conditions for rigorous learning	Develop expert learners	Personalise and connect learning
▶ Developing democratic relationships ▶ Building a community of learners ▶ Negotiating learning ▶ Supporting and challenging students to be successful	▶ Teaching students how to learn ▶ Fostering deep understanding ▶ Exploring the construction of knowledge ▶ Promoting dialogue as a means of learning	▶ Building on learners' understandings ▶ Connecting learning to student's lives and aspirations ▶ Applying and assessing learning in authentic contexts ▶ Communicating learning in multiple modes

A recent phase of this work has led South Australia to create professional learning communities of the kind we describe on pages 110 to 120.

Queensland

Between 2003 and 2008, the Queensland New Basics project sought to rethink the way educational outcomes were then thought about by more explicitly connecting them to activities that have an obvious connection to the real world—the third of our facets of expansiveness. The project also developed a useful knowledge base of pedagogical tools, which we refer to in Chapter 4.

Tasmania

Perhaps one of the most interesting stories of an attempt to introduce expansive education into Australia can be found in the development of the Tasmanian

Essential Learnings. It is a tale of enthusiasm, fearfulness, politics, teacher conservatism and a misunderstanding of the processes of habit change, from which all expansive educators might like to learn. Grant Rodwell has written up the whole episode and here we quote from the author's own scene-setting at the start of his article:

> In 2000, Paula Wriedt, the Tasmanian Minister for Education, gave instructions for her department to begin the development of a K to 10 statewide curriculum, soon to become known as the Essential Learnings Framework. The curriculum was an integrated one, doing away with traditional subjects, or disciplines, such as mathematics, science, English and history, and replacing these with an integrated, enquiry-based curriculum underpinned by constructivist pedagogy. This was the first attempt in Tasmania at a statewide K to 10 curriculum, and the first attempt at major system-wide curriculum change for nearly twenty years. Essentially, ELs was a political as much as an educational initiative.
>
> Following six years of intense public outrage and hostile public discourse, its demise closely followed the failed political fortunes of its political architect—Paula Wriedt. The ELs saga had far-reaching implications, going beyond simply the curriculum content and pedagogy for Tasmanian schools.[20]

An example from Australia of a broadly competence-based approach, drawing on Building Learning Power, is Bankstown Girls' High School in Sydney.

School case study: Bankstown Girls' High School

Bankstown Girls' High School is a good example of a school that has combined elements of home-grown innovation with thinking about the development of learning dispositions, pedagogical approaches and teacher enquiry.

Bankstown Girls' High School is a comprehensive government school in a south-western suburb of Sydney, Australia, catering for approximately 620 girls from Years 7 to 12. The Bankstown community is of low socioeconomic and high non-English-speaking background, which is reflected in the school population—98% of the girls have English as a second language and low-level literacy and numeracy skills when they first arrive at the school.

At Bankstown Girls', literacy and numeracy teaching projects have focused on developing thinking skills, student independence and, more recently, developing student capacity to transfer skills and knowledge across curriculum areas and into life beyond school. Although each of these projects produced improved student outcomes across all year groups and curriculum areas, especially for the lower ability students, teachers were concerned by the failure of many students, particularly those with higher ability, to apply skills and knowledge in different contexts or to have the confidence to persevere with tasks. It was like they knew how, but something prevented them from going beyond a certain point in their learning.

In 2011, the principal attended a conference where Bill Lucas talked about Building Learning Power (BLP), and she was struck by the similarity between this approach and that of her school. She especially noted what seemed to be the answer to her teachers' questions about the barriers to students extending their learning.

The Centre for Real-World Learning's pedagogy framework (an earlier version of what now appears on page 136) made sense to the school's pedagogy team and provided a way for teachers to consolidate all they had learned into a tool to analyse their classes and strategies. Further to this, the school's pedagogy team developed the Learning Powered Classroom program, through federal government funding. This program centred on developing teacher learning of the four core BLP learning dispositions—resilience, resourcefulness, reciprocity and reflectiveness—in themselves, in their teaching practice and then in their students. Using the information gathered through reciprocal observations, team discussions and school walk-throughs, teachers and teams learned to identify both the opportunities teachers provided for students to practice and develop their learning dispositions, and also how to best apply the teaching strategies to their students. The core group of teachers who initially trialled applying the dispositions in their classes now form the school's central professional learning community, with each member being a Leading Learner for a range of school Professional Learning Teams across the school. This approach is based on genuinely changing teacher practice through professional dialogue, teacher-generated action research, quality professional feedback and a cycle of evaluation.

One powerful example of changed teacher practice is evident in this snapshot of a Year 7 lesson taught by two of the Leading Learner teachers, Dragica Rapic, an English teacher, and Dianne Haselden, who teaches science. Both teachers had spent time observing each other's lessons and providing feedback around building students' learning habits. In English, the students were developing the metalanguage necessary to discuss and explain the literary devices and structural elements required in the construction of a paragraph, working towards the creation of an extended response. Dragica wanted the girls to utilise information learned within their science classroom, to make the necessary links to a film study, to incorporate factual information learned in other curriculum areas and to effectively apply them within a structured paragraph framework.

Through extensive dialogue with her colleague Dianne, the teachers devised a 'split screen' lesson, where both teachers taught the lesson, emphasising relevant cross-curriculum links and facilitating ways in which the students could logically organise and transfer learning from one situation to another, fostering reciprocity. As the English lesson dealt with issues pertaining to the Cold War from a thematic perspective, Dianne provided a scientific viewpoint by giving a brief presentation of the atomic age. Students were then instructed to consolidate this information and effectively incorporate it into their work describing the culture of fear and paranoia during the Cold War, by supporting their assertions through the necessary inclusion of factual (scientific) evidence.

Dragica then divided students into four groups and asked them to organise previously collated information using political and artistic critical frameworks. Dianne encouraged students to look at their science books for relevant cross-curriculum information. The girls were required to independently apply their new-found knowledge on paragraph-writing and the incorporation of factual evidence.

Dragica and Dianne assigned roles to girls within each group structure, as a way to foster self-management. Throughout the lesson, Dragica and Dianne asked students to refer to the 'stuck' poster on display in the classroom, with instructions to encourage them to be resilient, as well as to prompt them to capitalise upon the resources they had at their disposal.

Students were able to understand the relevance and interconnectedness of knowledge and the applicability of literacy strategies across all curriculum areas through the development of a joint metalanguage between the English and science content. Carefully planned group structures allowed student learning extension, encouraged dialogue and acknowledged individual learning needs and preferences.

At a national level, New Zealand has adopted a broadly expansive view of the desirable outcomes of school.

Example: The New Zealand National Curriculum

The New Zealand curriculum identifies five key competencies, which it calls 'capabilities for living and lifelong learning'. The description of the process by which these key competencies are developed is particularly illuminating:

> People use these competencies to live, learn, work, and contribute as active members of their communities. More complex than skills, the competencies draw also on knowledge, attitudes, and values in ways that lead to action. They are not separate or stand-alone. They are the key to learning in every learning area.[21]

The five 'capabilities for living and lifelong learning' are:

- thinking
- using language, symbols and texts
- managing self
- relating to others
- participating and contributing.[22]

A closer look at one of these five capabilities—managing self—indicates the expansive mindset guiding the New Zealand Curriculum:

> This competency is associated with self-motivation, a 'can-do' attitude, and with students seeing themselves as capable learners. It is integral to self-assessment. Students who manage themselves are enterprising, resourceful, reliable, and resilient. They establish personal goals, make plans, manage projects, and set high standards. They have strategies for meeting challenges. They know when to lead, when to follow, and when and how to act independently.

As its Foreword makes clear, the New Zealand Curriculum 'takes as its starting point a vision of ... young people as lifelong learners who are confident and creative, connected, and actively involved'.[23] The five competencies state that students need to be:

▶ confident
  ▶ positive in their own identity
  ▶ motivated and reliable
  ▶ resourceful
  ▶ enterprising and entrepreneurial
  ▶ resilient
▶ connected
  ▶ able to relate well to others
  ▶ effective users of communication tools
  ▶ connected to the land and environment
  ▶ members of communities
  ▶ international citizens
▶ actively involved
  ▶ participants in a range of life contexts
  ▶ contributors to the wellbeing of New Zealand—social, cultural, economic, and environmental
▶ lifelong learners
  ▶ literate and numerate
  ▶ critical and creative thinkers
  ▶ active seekers, users and creators of knowledge
  ▶ informed decision makers.[24]

A recently built school in Auckland shows how a determined school leader operating an expansive national framework such as New Zealand's curriculum can create a truly expansive school.

School case study: Stonefields School

Stonefields School was established in 2011 and started with 48 students aged between 5 and 13 years and has rapidly grown to 250 students in two years. The school is located in the heart of a new housing development called Stonefields in central Auckland, New Zealand. The student population currently represents over twenty cultures. This creates a necessity to be culturally responsive and inclusive.

The school's philosophy rests on four key principles: Building Learning Capacity, Collaborating, Making Meaning and Breaking Through. The focus on developing learners' capacity to thrive in tricky situations—knowing what to do when they don't know what to do—is valued highly. Teachers explicitly teach learners strategies to get out of 'I'm stuck' situations. Being stuck is celebrated and harnessed as an opportunity to build each individual's learning capacity.

Seven learner dispositions were co-constructed with staff prior to the opening of the school, and are now integrated into all learning. They are the dispositions to Reflect, Question, Connect, Think, Be Self-Aware, Wonder and Be Determined. The learner dispositions are key to building resilience in learners to ensure they proactively advance their own learning, can problem-find and problem-solve creatively and face their changing future with confidence. Key to embedding this learning has been making it visible in many different ways. All the children know the names and the symbols for each of their learning capacities, and can use them constructively to help to guide their own independent learning.

A target group of 25 students has been filmed every 6 months over the last 2 years and asked various questions to gauge how internalised their learning dispositions are and how well the four vision principles are understood. Questions asked include 'What makes a successful learner a successful learner?' and 'What do you do when you get stuck in your learning?' Two years ago, students' responses were very superficial and talked mainly about doing what the teachers said, listening or sitting quietly on the mat. The students were passive and behaved as if learning was something that happened to them rather than something they did. Two years on, learners across all year levels possess a powerful language for learning. They can talk about themselves as learners, describe how they apply the learner dispositions in various situations giving specific examples and reflect on what learner dispositions they need to further develop.

The Learner Disposition Continuum shown below serves as a guide to highlight where the students are and strategically informs the school's next steps.

Video summaries of students talking about themselves as learners are put on the school website to share with the wider community. School reports to parents describe their child's ability to name, describe, apply and internalise the learner dispositions. This evidence is quantified to inform the school's strategic direction.

Table 3.3 Stonefields School Learner Disposition Continuum

	Definition	Stage 0: Not yet	Stage 1: Developing	Stage 2: Proficient	Stage 3: Breakthrough
Questions	A way of finding out	I don't ask many questions	I can ask 'shallow' questions	I use a wider range of questions—'shallow' and 'deep'—to get information	I constantly ask questions to seek further information and deepen understandings
Reflection	Thinking about and looking back on the learning to decide how it went and where to next	I am not sure what reflection is or what it means	I reflect on my learning with support or prompts—e.g. question starters	I know reflection is an important part of the learning process. I can talk about when, what and how I reflect	I understand reflection helps me with my learning. I use it continuously across a range of situations
Thinking	Reasoning about, reflecting or pondering	I don't think much during my learning	With support I can use thinking organisers and strategies to further my learning.	I use various thinking tools and strategies to deepen my thinking and learning	I naturally select the most appropriate thinking tool and strategy to reach a desired decision, outcome, solution or situation I am faced with
Connections	Linking knowledge together to create new understandings	I am unable to make connections or links	I can sometimes make connections, often with support or modelling. Sometimes I have an 'ah ha' moment and I see a link or connection	I make many links and connections between pieces of knowledge to create new ideas or deeper understandings	I constantly look for and use knowledge to connect with old and new learning to develop new understandings

Table 3.3 (continued)

	Definition	Stage 0: Not yet	Stage 1: Developing	Stage 2: Proficient	Stage 3: Breakthrough
Determination	The ability to stick at a challenging task when you feel like giving up. The desire and determination to self improve and succeed	If things are too tricky I often give up	I can self-talk to show determination with tasks that are a little tricky and motivate myself to keep going	I have a number of strategies that help me to be determined when tasks are challenging	I am determined to self improve to achieve my very best. I choose from a range of strategies to overcome obstacles and problem-solve. I identify and commit to achieving next learning steps
Self-awareness	Aware of yourself as a learner—your actions, thoughts, strengths and next steps	I am not sure of the things that might help me to become a better learner	I am beginning to build awareness of what I need to do to become a better learner. I can identify some next steps to improve	I am self-aware in my actions and reflection to further improve and develop my strengths. I independently work towards achieving my next steps	I am conscious of what makes me 'tick' (strengths, next steps, thoughts and personality traits). I am self-motivated and self-aware of actions I need to improve as a learner
Wonder	To be amazed at something; the desire to know something	I am not sure what it means to wonder	I sometimes wonder and imagine	I can wonder about ideas and imagine possibilities from one or two perspectives	I wonder to come up with ideas about what 'might be' from many different perspectives. I can elaborate these ideas and come up with an original idea. I can distinguish between wonderings I can act on, and wonderings that are unobtainable

How to best capture children's progress in areas that have traditionally not been measured is an ongoing exploration. For example, when inquiring into the concept of collaboration, learners were interviewed to gain baseline data about their existing behaviour. Teachers then filmed a sample group of learners and tracked this group over time. This evidence and data is recorded in a Google site and is used to plan next steps for the learning and is also used to report to stakeholders, including the Board of Trustees.

Stonefields' Principal, Sarah Martin, reflects:

> We have learned that you need to remain courageous and not defer to the status quo. This is challenging work for our teachers, which requires honest reflection and continuous inquiry. Ongoing wondering, questioning, evidence and review informs our organisation's every step. We continue to learn significantly by listening carefully to our learners— reviewing videos of the children talking about their experiences and what would work better for them. We keep asking ourselves: 'What learning really matters for them in the 21st century?' We are determined to address what knowledge and competencies will help our learners cope and embrace a future of opportunity and uncertainty.

Across New Zealand, Learning Network NZ is an example of a leadership organisation actively trying to bring expansive approaches such as Building Learning Power, Habits of Mind, Philosophy for Children and Thinking Skills to schools on both the North and the South Islands. Learning NZ's approach is to bring the originators of many of the expansive education initiatives mentioned in this book to New Zealand and offer professional development for schools inspired by expansive thinking.

In the United Kingdom, the RSA (or as its full title has it, the Royal Society for the Encouragement of Arts, Manufactures and Commerce), an influential third-sector organisation, has been developing competence-based approaches for more than a decade.

Example: RSA Opening Minds

The RSA Opening Minds (OM) competence-based approach was first developed by the RSA in 2000 in response to concerns that young people were being educated in ways that had become increasingly detached from their needs as creative, resilient learners, citizens and employees in the real world of the 21st century. OM has five core competences, which seek to challenge curriculum models based on the transmission of content and information from teacher to pupils, preferring to encourage collaborative and integrated work. The five competences are:

1. citizenship
2. learning
3. managing information
4. relating to people
5. managing situations.

More than 200 secondary schools in the United Kingdom have adopted some aspects of the OM approach and recently the RSA decided to sponsor the RSA Academy in Tipton in the West Midlands. The RSA Academy is dedicated to implementing curriculum based on OM and also hosts a centre of excellence for the better understanding of OM. The RSA Academy is a member of the Expansive Education Network. As part of its professional development program, RSA has been using action research to understand more about the ways in which competence-based curricula can enhance teaching and learning.[25]

In a review of the OM program[26], Judy Sebba and colleagues make a number of helpful observations, which shed light on the development of more expansive approaches. These include:

- the need to recognise that different stakeholders have different views of which competences matter
- an over-reliance on standardisation
- the need to develop new approaches to assessment
- changing roles and identities for teachers, with the need to develop a more coaching style; being less of a subject expert and more of a facilitator.

Finland is often justifiably held up as an example of a high-attaining nation. Here we focus on the expansive processes by which such enviable success is achieved. Starting many places lower down in the educational rankings in the 1970s, Finland has systematically built up its school system so that its students regularly achieve outstanding results at the same time as maintaining some core expansive principles.

Ministry of Education case study: Finland

Finland achieves extraordinary success in external measures such as the Programme for International Student Assessment (PISA). It has done this not through top-down accountability initiatives, but through an emphasis on rigorous understandings of learning to learn approaches and on developing excellent teachers with an outstanding grasp of pedagogy. Indeed, Finland abolished inspections in the 1990s and replaced them with strong local self-evaluation, coupled with national evaluation systems.

Pasi Sahlberg, Director General of the Centre for International Mobility and Cooperation in Helsinki, stresses how this has been achieved by 'encouraging teachers and schools to continue to expand their repertoires of teaching methods and individualizing teaching to meet the needs of all students'.[27]

The philosophy of the Finnish education system is encapsulated by some telling headings and phrases in its booklet *Finnish education in a nutshell*, of which the following give a flavour:

▶ lifelong learning
▶ education system based on trust and responsibility
▶ assessment is part of daily schoolwork
▶ competence-based qualifications offer a way to demonstrate prior learning.[28]

Enquiry is at the core of Finnish approaches to pedagogy, with students playing a significant role in determining their own learning pathways. The dispositions of independence and active learning are deliberately cultivated and students develop metacognitive skills to help them think about and solve problems.

Teachers are encouraged to experiment with new teaching and learning methods and to reflect on the impact of their experiments. Indeed, the profession of teaching is framed as a research-based career—in their initial training, teachers are taught research methods and throughout their working lives they undertake enquiry and action research.

● ●

In this school example from Finland, you get a sense of a dynamic learning environment with many imaginative ways of developing competencies.

School case study: Koulumestari School and Innokas Learning Centre

Koulumestari School is a public primary school with 325 students (Classes 1–6, ages 7–12) located in Espoo, Finland. The school's overall aim is to support the learning of 21st century skills and competencies that will be needed in work and play in 2050. Innovative and creative thinking are an important part of these competencies and are essential in a technology-based society. The school hosts a national learning centre, Innokas ('eager' or 'pumped up' in English), which promotes creativity and innovations in learning. Innovation typically focuses on the use of Information and Communication Technology (ICT) in education. Innokas also provides nationwide guidance and in-service training for teachers and participates in educational development and research activities.

Almost 25% of Koulumestari students have special educational needs, and each one of these students has an individual education plan. The special-needs students are integrated with other students throughout the school. Special-needs and regular class teachers work together to devise the daily activities.

The school has a specific room, the 'innovation lab', set up with tools and materials that students can use to innovate and produce their own technological creations. As an example, a group of students may define their own problem, generate alternatives for the possible solution and combine and evaluate the solutions. Following this, the students are encouraged to innovate on new products based on the concept they've just learnt, as well as to combine other concepts into their new innovations.

The school makes extensive use of newly available robotics tools to encourage students to create and innovate. The students first learn the basics of robotics and programming and build and customise their first simple robot.

Then they are guided into assignments which encourage them to use more creativity and which require more problem-solving skills. For example, they might try to create and build a dancing robot (perhaps with the RoboCup Junior dancing contest as their future goal), which then needs to be clothed, have accompanying music selected and to be integrated with human performers.

This innovative way of working has been extended to the school's processes and the teachers' work. The school has three principals working as a team, each with their own areas of responsibility. The teachers are also organised into teams that take care of certain areas of the school's daily work. As a workplace, the school tries to encourage participation, openness and interaction. One practical example of this is the ongoing bi-monthly series of 'Pedagogical Cafés'. In these informal settings, teachers share their experiences and ideas on using innovation and technology in their teaching and student guidance.

Koulumestari also aims to create a wider culture to support the development of creativity and innovation in its students. The school sees expansive education as involving the increasing integration of teachers, leadership, school processes, parents and community partners in a way that enables this goal to be achieved. A web-based platform enables parents to engage with their children's creative activities and take an active part in supporting their child. For example, one parent commented:

> We've had some awesome moments when our child has shown their work on Opit [the web platform]—something which we would have never seen without this system—children do not normally mention such things at home but when they come up on the system they like to talk about them. It really warms your heart to see this thing.

The school's deputy head teacher, Tiina Korhonen, reflecting on the school's journey, said:

> We have learned that in order to develop the school you need to work simultaneously on multiple aspects, be patient and plan for the long term. The keys are to make sure everybody is brought into the activities, to get them excited about what we are doing and to make sure they know their contributions are valued! This includes the students, teachers and parents but also school administration and community stakeholders. Going forward, we intend to encourage other schools to also make use

of innovation, technology and collaboration in our school on various trainings and events organised through the learning centre, Innokas.

....

Developing key dispositions

There is much to learn from the Finnish approach, which demonstrates the importance of patience, commitment and innovation. Similarly, Singapore shows us that it is possible to achieve outstanding results and espouse truly expansive approaches. Regularly held up as a model of a high-performance education system, Singapore offers an unambiguously expansive framework.

Ministry of Education case study: Singapore

The person who is schooled in the Singapore education system embodies the desired outcomes of education. He has a good sense of self-awareness, a sound moral compass, and the necessary skills and knowledge to take on challenges of the future. He is responsible to his family, community and nation. He appreciates the beauty of the world around him, possesses a healthy mind and body, and has a zest for life. In sum, he is:

▶ A confident person who has a strong sense of right and wrong, is adaptable and resilient, knows himself, is discerning in judgment, thinks independently and critically, and communicates effectively
▶ A self-directed learner who takes responsibility for his own learning, who questions, reflects and perseveres in the pursuit of learning
▶ An active contributor who is able to work effectively in teams, exercises initiative, takes calculated risks, is innovative and strives for excellence
▶ A concerned citizen who is rooted to Singapore, has a strong civic consciousness, is informed, and takes an active role in bettering the lives of others around him.

In recent years the balance of teaching has shifted to reduce the amount of subject matter taught and to increase the learning of life-long skills, the building of character and competencies such as critical thinking and creativity.[29]

....

In the last few lines, the direction is spelled out with clarity. Schools that wish to become more expansive need to shift the balance of activities away from coverage and subject content towards the acquisition of certain key dispositions.

We believe that developing character or becoming a better person have been part of the goals of most schools for many years. But as expansive educators, we would want to qualify an assumption that the development of character is, per se, likely to be a proxy for expansive education. We think that it is not. Indeed, it is perfectly possible to conceive of a school taught on traditional lines, which bred compliant, helpless, dependent learners who were also of good character.

Project-based learning

Schools using a competence-based approach often end up adopting methods which are described as 'project-based' because their curricula are organised around topics, projects or enquiries rather than around subjects. Project-based learning can be deeply rigorous, authentic and motivating or well-intentioned but contrived, and not able to stretch the talents of those who are involved sufficiently. It can be confused with or contain elements of problem-based learning and enquiry-based learning. Project-based learning is helpfully defined by John Thomas:

> *Project-based learning (PBL) is a model that organizes learning around projects ... complex tasks, based on challenging questions or problems, that involve students in design, problem-solving, decision making, or investigative activities; give students the opportunity to work relatively autonomously over extended periods of time; and culminate in realistic products or presentations.*[30]

Learning Futures, a pioneering founding member of the Expansive Education Network, has researched and written a helpful guide to project-based learning, *Work that matters: the teacher's guide to project-based learning.*[31] Three 'keys' emerge as critical success factors of effective project-based learning:

1. **Exhibitions.** 'When students know that the work they are creating in a project will be displayed publicly, this changes the nature of the project from the moment they start working—because they know they will need to literally "stand by" their work, under scrutiny and questioning from family, friends and total strangers.'[32]
2. **Multiple drafts.** Ron Berger[33], Chief Programme Officer at Expeditionary Learning (whose work we describe on page 100), explains why this is so important: 'In most schools, students turn in first drafts—work that doesn't represent their best effort and that is typically discarded after it has been graded and returned. In life, when the quality of one's work really matters, one almost never submits a first draft. An ethic of excellence requires revision'.[34]
3. **Critique.** 'Formal critique sessions give students the opportunity to learn from each other's work and from each other's feedback in a structured, safe context.'[35]

These three critical success factors are almost always there in effective expansive education. As well as the learning being authentic, engaging, connected and exploratory, it is encouraging the dispositions of inquiry, collaboration, perseverance, reflectiveness, craftsmanship and so on. In Chapter 4 we explore the implications of these kinds of tools in building our approach to expansive pedagogy.

Blurring the boundaries

Sometimes the stimulus for thinking beyond subjects comes from divergent thinkers who refuse to see the differences between their subjects and prefer, instead, to focus on what they have in common. The Leonardo Effect[36] is a good example of just such collaboration, between science and art. Their approach is to:

> *use science and art as the catalyst to inspire learners to think, actively participate and have a voice in their own learning. It results in curriculum coherency, which is meaningful and relevant in the eyes of learners.*[37]

In terms of expansive education, this approach values certain dispositions common to both art and science such as investigating, imagining, developing ideas and creativity. Supported by St Mary's University College, Belfast, primary schools in Northern Ireland, Scotland, Wales and England have all found positive impacts on student learning when employing this kind of cross-curriculum collaboration. Ynstawe Primary School in Wales, one of the pilot schools for the Leonardo Effect, told us that: 'Children's motivation to learn is very high, creativity is promoted and their imaginations are developed. The approach is explorative and challenging and standards are clearly raised'. Welsh accountability body Estyn specifically commented on how Ynstawe Primary School had managed to make these approaches relevant for all children.

The Centre for Science Education[38] is a spin-off body from the Sheffield Hallam University and, like the Leonardo Effect, seeks to take an expansive approach to the teaching of science. Specifically, the Centre has explored the notion of scientific capability and the connections between those capabilities inherent in scientific enquiry with those more normally considered to be personal dispositions. The Centre is a founding pioneer member of the Expansive Education Network.

Assessment

There are three interesting models that start from the perspective of assessment: the International Baccalaureate, the International Primary Curriculum and ASDAN.

Example: International Baccalaureate

The International Baccalaureate (IB) was established in Geneva, Switzerland in 1968 as a not-for-profit educational foundation by a number of progressive and internationally minded teachers. Originally based in private international schools and designed to create a common pre-university experience for internationally mobile students, it now has as many government as private schools undertaking its curriculum. The IB is used in more than 3000 schools spread across 144 countries.[39]

The IB is expansive in terms of its aspirations for the wider goals of education, as can be seen from its stated aim: 'At our heart we are motivated by a mission to create a better world through education', further developed in its mission statement:

> The International Baccalaureate aims to develop inquiring, knowledgeable and caring young people who help to create a better and more peaceful world through intercultural understanding and respect.
>
> To this end the organization works with schools, governments and international organizations to develop challenging programmes of international education and rigorous assessment.
>
> These programmes encourage students across the world to become active, compassionate and lifelong learners who understand that other people, with their differences, can also be right.[40]

At the core of the IB are ten desirable qualities called the IB Learner Profile:

▶ inquisitive (independent, enthusiastic and skilful learners)
▶ knowledgeable (broad and deep understanding of important issues and ideas)
▶ thoughtful (critical, creative and rational in approaching complex issues)

- communicative (clear and confident in expressing ideas and in collaborating)
- principled (honest, trustworthy and respectful in interacting with others)
- open-minded (interested in and respectful of the ideas of many kinds of people)
- caring (kind and understanding in their dealings with others)
- risk-taking (confident to deal with uncertainty and explore new ideas)
- balanced (knowing when and how to adopt different attitudes appropriately)
- reflective (self-aware and honest about their strengths and limitations).

One study of the IB's implementation in three schools in Australia showed how the choice of the IB helped to 'level the playing field, helping students to realise their potential on grounds of meritocracy not socioeconomic background'.[41]

• •

In a parallel development, British organisation Fieldwork Education has created the International Primary Curriculum (IPC).

Example: International Primary Curriculum

The IPC is predicated on three questions, concerning the uncertainty of the world in the future, the kinds of dispositions children will need to succeed and the kinds of learning they need to acquire. The IPC describes itself as 'a comprehensive, thematic, creative curriculum for 3–11 year olds, with a clear process of learning and with specific learning goals for every subject, for international mindedness and for personal learning'.[42]

The IPC personal goals are clearly expansive:

> Those individual qualities and dispositions we believe children will find essential in the 21st century. They help to develop those qualities that will enable children to be at ease with the continually changing context of their lives. There are personal goals for enquiry, resilience, morality, communication, thoughtfulness, cooperation, respect and adaptability.[43]

As an example, the IPC personal goal for adaptability is as follows. Children, through their study of the IPC, will learn to:

- ▶ know about a range of views, cultures and traditions
- ▶ be able to consider and respect the views, cultures and traditions of other people
- ▶ be able to cope with unfamiliar situations
- ▶ be able to approach tasks with confidence
- ▶ be able to suggest and explore new roles, ideas, and strategies
- ▶ be able to move between conventional and more fluid forms of thinking
- ▶ be able to be at ease with themselves in a variety of situations.[44]

The IPC is now used in more than a thousand schools across the world.

••

Our next example, ASDAN, grew out of the efforts of pioneering teachers and university researchers. ASDAN was a deliberate attempt to provide an antidote for the subject-based national curriculum being introduced in England and Wales in the 1980s. ASDAN originally stood for Award Scheme Development and Accreditation Network but the organisation has dropped this longer title in favour of the more memorable acronym.

Example: ASDAN

ASDAN is a curriculum development organisation and awarding body, offering programs and qualifications that explicitly grow skills for learning, skills for employment and skills for life. Developed and managed by practitioners, ASDAN grew out of research work at the University of the West of England and was formally established as an educational charity in 1991.

ASDAN specifically provides opportunities for capabilities learned outside schools to be recognised through its Certificate of Personal Effectiveness (CoPE), a qualification outcome of the ASDAN programs. CoPE is a portfolio of evidence that is built by students and of use to themselves, their teachers and potential employers.

> The qualifications offer imaginative ways of accrediting young people's activities. They promote, and allow centres to record, a wide range of personal qualities, abilities and achievements of young people, as well as introducing them to new activities and challenges.[45]

Research undertaken by the University of the West of England has shown a direct positive impact on public examination results at age 16 in England for those students taking part in CoPE. 10% more students achieved a C+ in English in the GCSE qualification. Even more remarkably, the chances of students from black and ethnic minority backgrounds who took part in CoPE achieving the benchmark C+ rose to 49%.[46]

As well as in England, ASDAN has centres across the world in countries as diverse as Australia, China, Singapore, the United States, Vietnam and Zimbabwe.

Stories from the frontline of expansive education: demonstrating the learnability of intelligence

Several times in this book we have touched on the work of Stanford University professor Carol Dweck and, in particular, her innovative thinking about the kinds of growth mindsets that motivate young people to achieve extraordinary results. Her writings have inspired us in our thinking over the last decade or so and are at the heart of the second aspect of our definition of expansive education: that intelligence is expandable.

Example: Mindset Works

Mindset Works is a social venture created by Carol Dweck and her colleague Lisa Sorich Blackwell. Mindset Works offers support to students, teachers and schools to learn and implement the growth mindset approach.

> The growth mindset, the understanding of intelligence and abilities as qualities we can develop, has been shown over and over to have powerful ramifications on student motivation and learning, and school success. When teachers and students focus on improvement rather than on whether they're smart, kids learn a lot more.[47]

Mindset Works provides professional development for educators, a program for students called Brainology and a 'SchoolKit' for schools to use, developed and tested for the United States Department of Education's Institute of Education Sciences.

Early results from the interventions of Mindset Works are very encouraging. Students who had developed a growth mindset outperformed their fixed mindset peers in mathematics.[48] In another study, also with adolescents, students were divided into two groups for a workshop on the brain and study skills. Half of them, the control group, were taught about the stages of memory; the other half received training in the growth mindset and how to apply this idea to their schoolwork. Three times as many students in the growth mindset group showed an increase in effort and engagement compared with the control group. After the training, the control group continued to show declining grades, but the growth-mindset group continued to improve their grades.[49]

These two pieces of research are part of a broader picture in which belief in a growth mindset leads to gains in both attainment *and* to the development of the kinds of expansive capabilities that we have been describing in this book.

• •

The Building Learning Power framework is fundamentally predicated on a shared belief in the power of growth mindsets and in a deep understanding of the kinds of dispositions for learning, which are both significant and learnable. It shares some approaches with the Habits of Mind movement described earlier on page 56 but, interestingly, both approaches were developed in isolation on either side of the Atlantic!

Example: Building Learning Power

Building Learning Power (BLP) is a detailed map for teachers and school leaders that will help them develop a strong culture of learning to learn in their schools and classrooms. Founded in 2002 by Guy Claxton, then Professor of Education at the University of Bristol, BLP derived from 30 years of research into the foundations of learning, and what made some people more powerful learners than others. The original book on BLP[50] offered teachers two frameworks for thinking about their teaching: a coherent map of the learning habits or dispositions that combine to create 'learning power' and a clear delineation of the variety of ways in which a teacher's behaviour in the classroom could influence the development of these dispositions.

Claxton's 'learning muscles', as he called them, included several that are familiar from other expansive approaches—resilience, imagination, collaboration, attentive noticing—as well as some that derive from recent research in the learning sciences such as 'intuition' and the judicious use of 'imitation'. BLP relies a good deal on a metaphor that relates 'learning power' to physical fitness. Learning power is a kind of 'mental fitness for life' that comprises a variety of different learning muscles, each of which can be strengthened through deliberate exercise. The classroom is a 'mind gym' where activities function like the different exercise machines in a real fitness centre. Students can struggle to achieve targets and exceed their 'personal bests' in resilience and concentration.

BLP's original focus was very much on the classroom, and on the kinds of habit change that would help teachers to create effective 'fitness centres' for the development of learning power. More recently, the approach has broadened out to include the development of a school-wide culture of curiosity and experimentation—among teachers and other members of staff, as well as among students.

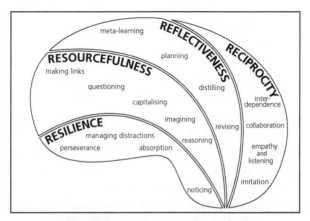

Figure 3.2 Your learning powered mind

The Learning Powered School,[51] has distilled the results of a detailed evaluation of 18 pioneering BLP schools into a third framework for helping school leaders chart their culture-change journey over a period of years, so that students systematically develop real-life learning power at the same time as they do as well as possible on more conventional tests.

BLP is a founding member of the Expansive Education Network.

••

Two school examples from opposite halves of the world exemplify how BLP is taking root. The first is from Argentina.

School case study: Kites Language School

Kites Language School is situated in Ushuaia, right at the southernmost tip of Argentina. Pupils between the ages of 4 and 18 come to the Institute after school to learn English, with the aim of leaving with a Cambridge First Certificate. Learning English at Kites has a huge impact on the future of these children as English teaching in mainstream schools is often poor and English is essential for university studies and most jobs in the local area's tourism industry.

Groups at Kites are small, with a maximum of 10 pupils, so learning is personalised and every learner is catered for. The school was previously called 'English Through Stories', reflecting the main approach of teaching children through exploring stories, poetry and song. Teachers at Kites have always sought new ways to teach pupils in meaningful ways, based on the latest studies into how children learn. In particular, they are very mindful of the learning habits they are embedding in their learners through the way they teach, the words they use and the attitudes to learning that they model to their pupils. Since Kites doesn't teach through worksheets and grammar exercises, which is the approach of most other English schools in the area, pupils aren't faced with lists of right and wrong answers. Instead, they are usually given feedback that encourages them to check progress for themselves. Becky Ensum, a teacher at Kites, commented, 'I have never experienced a child being scared of making a mistake in Kites—I am not sure they would even understand why anyone would feel ashamed of being wrong!'

Teaching at Kites help students understand the characteristics of a powerful language learner, and how each one of them can develop their own learning power. For example, groups of students may be encouraged to develop their own list of learning dispositions, give examples and talk about how they link together. Once they have this working vocabulary, they might write the dispositions they came up with on cards and use these to discuss which ones they would need for each part of the lesson. They might choose the words 'collaboration', 'open-mindedness' and 'positive attitude to mistakes' when they were peer-marking each others' written work; then 'absorption' and 'independence' when they were doing a writing activity.

With one class, Becky created a scale of challenge that went from 'Easy-peasy lemon squeezy' to 'rock hard'. (The students loved the 'slang' they were learning—Becky says she lost count of the times she heard them saying 'easy-peasy lemon squeezy' and laughing to themselves.) She noticed that they started spontaneously to reflect on their level of English and to show greater relish for a challenge. They began to see that they could play with their English and make it more interesting and not just say the first thing that came to their head. For example, they went from using simple questions like, 'Where is the hotel?' to grammatically more difficult questions such as, 'Would you mind telling me where the hotel is?' More importantly, it affected their self-esteem as learners: they felt great when they tried something 'rock hard'. Several of them were heard proudly telling their parents they had done something 'rock hard'— of course, their parents wondered what on earth they were talking about!

The teachers created a colour-coded marking system. Each colour gave the students a clue as to what their mistake might have been, but they had to work out exactly what it was and how to change it. The pupils enjoyed the challenge of noticing and correcting their own mistakes. There was a discussion about 'silly mistakes' and 'good mistakes'—the former being mistakes students made from not paying attention and the latter being mistakes made when taking a risk. One of their feedback codes was yellow, which meant 'could be'. It signalled that the way they had translated something was fine, but they might be able to think of several other ways of saying the same thing. This created a demonstrably greater feeling of playfulness and adventure in their writing. Becky found that these kinds of techniques really opened pupils up to give things a go and also expanded their English vocabulary.

Overall, teachers were convinced that these kinds of small changes had a surprisingly big impact on pupils' attitudes to and enjoyment of learning as well as their confidence in the class. But they discovered that making sure that they were embedded in everyday classroom practice required real commitment. As Becky said, 'It can be difficult to not let things tail off and to keep the momentum going.'

••

The second BLP case study comes from rural England.

School case study: Nayland Primary School

Nayland is a small but growing school in rural Suffolk, one year into its transition from being a 'first school' (for three- to eight-year-olds) to becoming a full primary (up to 11 years old). Based on Building Learning Power, Nayland's philosophy constantly seeks to help children become confident and creative lifelong learners, readying them for everything the world has to throw at them. Raegan Delaney's thirteen years as Head and her passion for BLP have brought two glowing Ofsted inspection reports, and just a few conversations with staff and students reveal the enthusiasm there is for the revolution over which she has presided. What is also clear is the impact it is having on even the youngest children's understanding of what going to school is all about.

'When I arrived it was already a good school,' Raegan says, 'but the children were sitting like little birds in a nest with their mouths open, and teachers were running around frantically feeding them learning worms. What the children weren't doing is what little birds all have to learn to do: get out there and find their own worms. Learning isn't just an outcome, it's a process. With children, you have to celebrate the struggle—and if it's not a struggle then they're not learning.'

Despite the relative complexity of some of the language and concepts BLP brings to the table, Raegan is clear about the benefits of catching children early. Helping even the youngest children get to grips with the idea of the differing 'learning muscles' are a quartet of puppets, one for each of the four Rs of Building Learning Power: Resourcefulness, Reflectiveness, Reciprocity—'Yes, the children can say that', Raegan says—and Resilience.

> Reflectiveness is the strength that comes from looking back on your learning and tweaking it as necessary. Reciprocity is about collaboration and listening and empathising with others. Resourcefulness is how you find things out—about being a questioner and using your imagination.

Resilience is about being up for a challenge, being able to manage your distractions and stick with your learning. Each R can be unpacked into a number of component capacities that expand its meaning. These are communicated to the children as they get older through a 'toolbox' containing a tool for each capacity, for example, a hammer representing 'perseverance' and a blindfold, which symbolises children's ability to 'manage their distractions'.

Nayland values progress in reading, writing, maths and so on—but it monitors students' development as confident learners as well. To Raegan, powerful learning and high attainment go hand in hand, and the school keeps a close watch on standards at all times. But 'alongside that,' she says, 'we talk a lot about how well each child is developing as a learner. In our reports, the first thing we mention is BLP. It might say something like "Eleanor has really developed her ability to work alongside others and is beginning to actively collaborate in class". And, if you read through the rest of the report, you'll find BLP is knitted in there as well'.

Ginny Day, Assistant Head and Reception teacher, is in no doubt about the effectiveness of BLP. 'The children have become more independent learners since we introduced BLP; they know how to find things out and organise learning for themselves. In the old days, you would be moving one child away from another because they were distracting each other; now it's the children making those decisions. They know where to sit to be a good learner.' Jane Kennedy, Year 4 class teacher and special educational needs coordinator, saw the difference in her own children as they progressed through Nayland. 'BLP was introduced to the school while my children were still pupils here. They would come home and talk about it, and it just made sense. There are so many philosophies out there and BLP brings them all together. It's not something that I feel is imposed; it's just a tool for teaching the children to manage learning for themselves.'

● ●

A number of organisations have adopted approaches to learning that stress enquiry and which have come to be grouped under the general title of 'Philosophy for Children'. These approaches have little time for the notion that, just because a child is younger, he or she cannot expand his or her horizons to think philosophically!

Example: Philosophy for Children

Originally created by Professor Matthew Lipman while at Columbia University in New York, in response to a belief that very young children were able to use abstract concepts and as a reaction to what Lipman saw as poor undergraduate reasoning and enquiry skills, Philosophy for Children (P4C) has gained currency in schools across the world. A key milestone was the International Council for Philosophical Inquiry with Children[52] in 1983, after a P4C workshop in Denmark. Since then, philosophical dialogue in communities of enquiry has been undertaken in schools in more than 60 countries.

Two key practices inform P4C: the whole thinking process is driven by enquiry and significant changes of thought and action are only achieved through reflection.

SAPERE[53], a charitable body in the UK providing and validating training as well as being a membership organisation, is a founding pioneer of the Expansive Education Network, and there are several other (often small) organisations providing training, resources and support to schools (such as Philosophy4Children[54] and The Philosophy Foundation[55]) in this area.

Several research studies have been undertaken into the impact of Philosophy for Children, all of which show gains in these three areas:

1. developments in cognitive ability such as reasoning ability
2. developments in critical reasoning skills and dialogue in the classroom with, for example, pupils better able to support their views with reasons and teachers better able to use open-ended questioning techniques
3. emotional and social developments including evidence of improvements in pupils' communication skills, confidence and concentration and suggestions that the process of enquiry helped pupils learn to self-manage their feelings and levels of impulsivity more appropriately.[56]

In parallel to this specific interest in the philosophical skills of enquiry and reflection there have been various longstanding and more broadly focused attempts to develop students' thinking skills in schools. Project Zero, whose seminal work we have already encountered on page 54, has done some of the most interesting work in this area. Here it is their notion of a thinking routine that is most helpful in making explicit the connection with expansive education. For, unless we understand the thinking routines and habits of mind that are modelled in classrooms, we will be unlikely truly to expand the purpose of education. Here's a very clear description of what is going on:

> *Routines exist in all classrooms; they are the patterns by which we operate and go about the job of learning and working together in a classroom environment. A routine can be thought of as any procedure, process, or pattern of action that is used repeatedly to manage and facilitate the accomplishment of specific goals or tasks. Classrooms have routines that serve to manage student behavior and interactions, to organize the work of learning, and to establish rules for communication and discourse. Classrooms also have routines that structure the way students go about the process of learning. These learning routines can be simple structures, such as reading from a text and answering the questions at the end of the chapter, or they may be designed to promote students' thinking, such as asking students what they know, what they want to know, and what they have learned as part of a unit of study.[57]*

Unless we become more mindful of what our chosen (or accidental) routines 'say' about our educational beliefs, we will never intentionally create a system predicated on expansive approaches.

One initiative has sought to fashion schools around quality thinking as the defining characteristic.

Example: Thinking Schools

A collaboration between a publishing and training organisation, Kestrel, and a well-respected research group, the Cognitive Education Centre at the University of Exeter, has created the idea of the 'Thinking School'.[58] This approach supports schools to adopt a whole-institution approach and embed tools and methods across all subjects.

As well as providing a range of training and consultancy services and offering a level of quality assurance to schools who are genuinely serious about cultivating thinking dispositions in students, Kestrel also regularly produce digests of useful research papers about the benefits of, lessons learned from and weaknesses of different approaches to promoting thinking skills.[59]

● ●

Across the world, there are many organisations espousing aspects of thinking in schools that come together to share ideas at international meetings. Such gatherings show that in many countries there is a range of local support organisations such as the ones we have exemplified as being active in the United Kingdom on pages xviii to xx.

Stories from the frontline of expansive education: going beyond the school

Thus far, our pioneering examples have been drawn mainly from our first two meanings of expansive education: organisations concerned to expand the goals of education beyond subjects into certain preferred dispositions for learning and life; and those that start with a deeply held belief that intelligence is expandable and seek to explore the practical implications for classrooms. Indeed, many of the organisations listed in one of these first two categories could have been featured in either or both.

We now explore some stories from beyond the school gates, from educators interested in learning in the real world, often through hands-on experiences with mentors other than teachers, or in fields such as sustainable development or by more directly engaging with parents. A cluster of organisations have taken learning in the wider community as their starting point and are exploring ways in which this third dimension of our definition of expansive education can develop young people's capabilities.

In Australia there is now a sister organisation to the Expansive Education Network, Expansive Learning Network.

Example: Expansive Learning Network

Australia's Expansive Learning Network (ELN) explicitly seeks to engage a broad range of stakeholders who are passionate about learning for the real world to work together to make the necessary changes to their practice. The website invites potential collaborators to:

▶ engage with thought leaders in tackling provocative propositions
▶ collaborate to deliver world-class 21st century education
▶ reap the benefits of closer connections between education providers and industry, to increase local and regional economic success
▶ create the conditions for innovation
▶ contribute to best practice through action research
▶ share the fruits of ELN's enquiries.[60]

ELN is both taking learning out of school and building a community of professional enquiry to reflect on and share experiences.

● ●

There are many examples globally of educators deliberately going outside the boundary of school. One such example in the United Kingdom is the aptly named Widehorizons Outdoor Education Trust[61] which focuses on the needs of urban children in the London boroughs of Greenwich and Lewisham and which owns and manages six outward bound centres in remoter parts of the United Kingdom. There are many similar models to this across the world.

In this broad mould, Expeditionary Learning in the United States is one approach that seems to hold useful lessons for expansive educators.

Example: Expeditionary Learning

Expeditionary Learning is another 'child' of the very expansively fecund Harvard Graduate School of Education (see Project Zero's entry on page 54). In 1987, the Harvard Outward Bound Project was established to increase the profile of experiential education and also to bring about increased academic rigour of this work in schools. Expeditionary Learning was created out of this thinking during the 1990s. Today, Expeditionary Learning has 165 schools in 29 states. The approach is summed up on the organisation's website:

> Expeditionary Learning schools inspire the motivation to learn, engage teachers, and students in new levels of focus and effort, and transform schools into places where students and adults become leaders of their own learning.[62]

The expansiveness of what is being promoted is clear:

> Our model fosters more than just academic engagement and achievement. Beyond developing critical thinking, problem-solving, and collaboration skills, our students show leadership through civic engagement and social and environmental service. Our teachers and school leaders are equally involved in their schools and communities.[63]
>
> Expeditionary Learning espouses a set of principles that includes supported self-discovery, the development of empathy, calculated risk-taking, blending collaboration with competitiveness and valuing experiences in the natural world. It is this latter aspect of learning outside school—direct engagement with nature—that many organisations are promoting across the world.[‡]

• •

Expansive exemplars

Our expansive exemplars in going beyond the classroom—Learning through Landscapes (LtL), Open Futures and the Eden Project, all in

---

‡ In the United Kingdom, a similar venture exists called Adventure Learning Schools: http://adventurelearningschools.org

the United Kingdom—are founding pioneer members of the Expansive Education Network.

LtL[64] promotes the development of school grounds as outdoor classrooms and places for play and social development. For nearly two decades, it has been supporting schools in designing, using and managing school grounds for more expansive learning opportunities.[65] Its supposition is that children learn differently and teachers teach differently where there is no 'desk'; in other words, when they are simply outdoors, engaged in some kind of activity. By learning outside the classroom, questioning, problem solving and collaborative working are all encouraged, along with high levels of engagement for most children.

Open Futures[66] looks outside the school with a more specific lens, encouraging children to grow food and make meals from what they have grown. At the same time, they promote enquiry and the use of film. This eclectic blend reduces to a memorable set of suggestions for schools: ask it, grow it, cook it, film it! Schools undertaking Open Futures activities report increased levels of engagement, good behaviour and social, practical and cognitive skills.[67]

Example: The Eden Project

The Eden Project is an extraordinary organisation. In the middle of Cornwall, its vast glass biomes recreate different world habitats and it is constantly, like the natural world, adapting and developing new features. Its creator, Sir Tim Smit, has legendary powers of resourcefulness, tenacity, creativity, energy and ingenuity and needed all of these to persuade investors to create this new Eden for our times in an old quarry. Perhaps unsurprisingly, Eden has many of these hallmarks, too. Its education program transcends schools and says simply:

We love to help people learn, including:

▶ adults looking to try something new or develop a hobby
▶ professionals wanting to build on skills or boost your business

▶ school, college and university students seeking an inspirational learning experience

▶ parents and teachers looking for new ways of engaging young people.[68]

Eden's focus is on outdoor learning—what it is, what kinds of methods work best and why it is important.

The Eden Project is a founding member of the Expansive Education Network and Smit is convinced that this kind of learning is important:

> The Expansive Education Network is to be applauded for bringing so many pioneering organisations together to help young people discover themselves and develop the appetites and interests that make for a rounded life. I wholeheartedly support it.[69]

Extended activities and interventions

In the United Kingdom, there is also an umbrella organisation—The Council for Learning Outside the Classroom[70]—that brings all such organisations together and seeks to analyse the benefits of this kind of learning. Of course, it is technically possible to teach outdoors in a way that invites students to sit passively on their spades and to work silently on unmotivating tasks, but it is much more likely that the teaching is dynamic, collaborative and engaging and that the habits of mind learned are about group collaboration, problem-solving and empathy for and care of the natural world. These examples are indicative of similar, if culturally and contextually different, approaches across the world.

As well as expanding spatially what is on offer at school, there are temporal opportunities, too. Extended schools or, as they are sometimes known, 'full-service schools' have existed in the United States since the 1930s. The original idea was to go beyond education to the provision of other services, such as healthcare, on the same site. A contemporary example is ExpandED Schools[71], established by The After-School Corporation (TASC). Primarily focusing on areas of deprivation and with an explicit intention of closing the attainment gap, ExpandED Schools offers a longer school day model, currently running in New York schools. Similar schemes have been adopted in the United Kingdom, starting in 1998, with aspects of expanded days and extended provision seeking in a very functional way to expand the role of school. Early examples of the work in the United Kingdom were evaluated and some of the findings may resonate for expansive educators, of which we highlight two:

> *Many projects have found that the development of extended schools is an important catalyst for enhancing collaboration between education and other agencies.*

> *It may be more productive to see extended activities as central to the role of every school (albeit to varying degrees) and a different funding model may need to be found to reflect this new understanding. In this case, there is the possibility of a real development in the way in which schools relate to their communities and set about educating their pupils.*[72]

Part of the motivation to move teaching and learning outside of school is often the sense that there may be more opportunities for real-world learning out there. Certainly, what it is to learn well in the real world is a core preoccupation of ours, especially when it comes to understanding practical learning. These concerns are shared by a small number of expansive educators globally.

A powerful example provided by an Australian organisation is Hands On Learning.

Example: Hands On Learning

Hands On Learning is the brain- or, should we say, hand-child of Russell Kerr.

Russell Kerr founded the program in October 1999 at Frankston High School in Victoria. The idea was conceived when Russell took 12 students into the Warburton Forest with a friend, skilled artisan Frank Wimmer, and two support staff. The students were taught how to find the right sticks, and on returning to Frank's backyard, were shown how to build a chair from their sticks.

There were no long instructions, no complicated technologies, just an opportunity to start doing—under skilled supervision. So a valuable lesson was learnt: approach tasks that are 'doable' and readily achievable—tasks that will lead to building self-confidence and self-esteem.[73]

Hands On Learning targets young people who are most at risk of dropping out of school in the middle years of their education, giving them a chance to have direct involvement in practical building projects—making a pizza oven, installing a boardwalk, building a shed, assembling bicycles for primary aged children—in their local community and work with sympathetic, motivated adults.

In areas where the program is used, youth unemployment levels are significantly lower than the national average, as are unexplained absences at school, while retention rates at school are higher.[74]

While Hands On Learning focuses on its chosen target groups of young people, it also acts as a lobbying group for the broader advocacy of practical learning in Australia.

• •

Embedded activities

Practical tasks in the community are one very specific kind of expansive out-of-school approach. But the method used begs the question as to whether, for many students, such approaches might be motivating and engaging if they were part of their overall school experience, rather than a special intervention.

School case study: DaVinci Academy

The DaVinci Academy is a charter school in Ogden, Utah. Originally the brainchild of a coalition of business, science, education and community leaders in early 2003, DaVinci seeks to provide the knowledge and skills students need in the 21st century. DaVinci Academy was chartered by the Utah State Board of Education and opened its doors in August 2004 with the mission of integrating science and the arts after the example of the original Renaissance man, Leonardo da Vinci. Subsequently, this has progressed into a college with a project-based curriculum that addresses the needs of the whole child.

According to its Founding Principal, Nicole Assisi, three core practices drive its work. DaVinci aims to integrate these three strands into all that it does.

First, its learn-by-doing model integrates project-based learning with real-life problem solving with many opportunities for students to critique and present their work and build up digital portfolios.

Second, its curriculum is based on a hybrid model of classroom-based and family-facilitated instruction. Families are seen as an integral part of their children's education and each child has a personalised learning plan agreed with parents.

Third, there is a deliberate attempt to cultivate certain habits of mind and heart, such as compassion, empathy, self-responsibility and collaboration. These are encouraged by much of the teaching being done in multi-age classrooms.

The core values of DaVinci draw from a powerful list of expansive dispositions—Citizenship, Competitiveness, Creativity, Compassion, Contemplation, Collaboration and Curiosity.

• •

Student-focused systems

The idea that practical learning is worthwhile, complex and intrinsically motivating is not, of course, new and there are schools across the world and many other catalytic organisations that work with these concepts in mind. We have written about the subject at some length[75] as have, for example, Ron Berger[76], Mike Rose[77], Matthew Crawford[78] and Richard Sennett.[79] But schools seem slow to see it as a central concern and part of their core purposes.

Another way in to expansive education is through the student. In Chapter 2 we saw how, for many progressive educators, putting the child at the centre of the system was an important preoccupation. The QED Foundation in the United States is a good contemporary example of an organisation seeking to explore what student-centredness means and how this might expand the experience of school.

Example: QED Foundation

QED Foundation[80] is a not-for-profit organisation that combines interests in student-centredness and the importance of certain key habits of mind with a belief in the capacity of all students to learn successfully. It was founded in 2007 based on work started in a competency-based high school program in the Monadnock Community Connections School in New Hampshire.[81]

QED is explicit about its theory of change:

▶ we create competency-based learning pathways and learning opportunities
▶ [we] know and embrace each student's strengths, challenges, passions and abilities
▶ [we] intentionally design for student agency, coaching and assessing habits of mind and being
▶ [we] cultivate communities of collaboration and partnership both inside and outside of school
▶ [we] embed these practices in laboratories of democratic practice.[82]

An advocacy group, QED seeks to increase demand, increase capacity and provide demonstration sites for others to learn from. It has developed a sophisticated model to describe the progression from 'traditional' to 'transformative'. Some (though not all) of the elements listed as 'transformational' are very much in the spirit of what we are describing as expansive.

In particular, the emphasis on teacher enquiry, on competency-based approaches with ongoing discussion about the process of learning and on more fundamental relationship with students and their families, we see overlap with the philosophy of education we are developing.

Figure 3.3 QED Transformational Change Model[83]

	Traditional	Transitional	Transformational
Model of success is based on	The willing and able	Inclusion	Racial and social justice
Educator development	Re-certification hours every three years	Group learning	Collaborative inquiry
Student investment	Requirements	Engagement	Passion
Academic access	Tracking	Open access to all	All students are successful at high levels
Curriculum implementation	Text-driven seat time	Standards-based instruction	Competency based
Driving the learning	Coverage	Depth and breadth	EQ and competency based inquiry
Curriculum frame	Scope and sequence	Tasks and projects	Whole child
Curriculum goals	Test results targets	College- and career-ready	Learner aspirations and life options
Feedback	Teacher corrects	Student reflects on learning	Ongoing discussion of learning
Assessment	... of learning	... for learning	... as learning
Reporting	Letter grades, GPA	No-zero grading	Proficiency reporting
Personalisation	Group instruction	Differentiation	Personalised learning plans
Student support	Deficit model	Response to intervention	Strengths, assets and learner profiles
'Accountability'	Student	Teacher	Learning team
Parent and student involvement	Parent–teacher conference	Student conferences	Student-led exhibitions/IEP meetings
Context for learning	Classroom	School	Community
Where and when learning happens	School (8 am–2 pm)	Coordination of in and after school	Anywhere and everywhere
Community contributions	Resources	Partners	Collaborators
Leadership	Hierarchy, defined by position	Sited-based, shared	Everyone takes responsibility for what matters
Governance	Student council	Representational democratic structures	Participatory democratic structures
Discipline	Rules and punishments	PBIS	Restorative practices
Culture	Compliance	Cooperation	Collaboration
Professional culture	Faculty meeting	Professional learning communities	Critical friends groups

Parents

There is one vital piece of the jigsaw, in our stories from organisations and schools that have sought to move beyond the school gates, on which we have hardly touched: parents.

A number of educators have shown just how much children and families benefit from genuine parental engagement in schools and how this can be done. In the United States, Joyce Epstein, Director of the Center on School, Family, and Community Partnerships, has created perhaps the most widely used typology[84] of six types of parent engagement to describe how this works. Other influential parent educators in the United States adopting more expansive approaches include Karen Mapp, Anne Henderson[85] and Heather Weiss.§ In the chart below[86], we draw on this and speculate as to how it might be if the engagement was explicitly expansive.

The National Network of Partnership Schools[87], created by Epstein and based at Johns Hopkins University, and the Harvard Family Research Project site[88] are two of the best repositories of well-researched resources we know.

In the United Kingdom, there has been a growing interest in the role of parents in education and their impact on student attainment, wellbeing and effectiveness as learners.[89] But while most teachers the world over know that it is important to involve and engage parents, there is still a reluctance in many countries for this to be wholeheartedly embraced. There are good examples of individual schools that have embraced the concept, but for our school example we include a chain of schools spread across the world.

School case study: GEMS Education

GEMS Education owns and runs some 100 schools across the world. Some are international schools, some are independent and local and some are public

---

§   Heather Weiss is the founding director of the Harvard Family Research Project.

Table 3.4 Expansive parent engagement

Epstein's six types of parent engagement		... and with an expansive education twist
Type 1: Parenting	Helping all families to have the basic home conditions in place, including active parenting strategies and regular communication with school	Helping all parents to become learning coaches and specifically to understand core principles of reward and praise strategies
Type 2: Communicating	Designing effective home-to-school and school-to-home communication methods, which engage all parents regularly	Designing effective engagement processes to enable all parents to understand that certain dispositions for life and learning are important and how they can be cultivated at home. Reconfiguring school reward and reporting structures in line with a belief in the power of growth mindsets
Type 3: Volunteering	Recruiting volunteer parents to help in school, in classes and in extra-curricular activities	Recruiting volunteer parents to act as Parent Learning Champions in school and within the parent body
Type 4: Learning at home	Providing good information to enable all parents to help with homework and offer other family learning activities	Rethinking homework to become a range of home learning activities designed to strengthen those habits of mind deemed to be most important and in support of learning undertaken at school
Type 5: Decision-making	Including parents in decision-making activities to build a sense of ownership, including being involved in governance	Including parents in decision-making activities to build a sense of ownership, including being involved in shaping the range of expansive learning experiences on offer
Type 6: Collaborating with community	Finding and using resources from the wider parent community to enrich school life	Creating a talent bank of parents or individuals with passion and enthusiasm who can be local learning heroes and coaches

schools. A large number are in the Middle East where, especially in Dubai, GEMS has developed a number of interesting ways of advancing, supporting and embedding robust approaches to parental engagement.

GEMS has created a dedicated website to support teachers and parents[90] and it holds an annual festival—Parental Engagement Week—every year in January. It has also developed the '3-a-day' concept, as a way for parents to support their children's learning through talking with, sharing and encouraging their child. GEMS has created an app for parents and teachers to use, giving prompts for activities and approaches. As it says on its website:

> The '3-a-day' approach gives parents clear and simple direction to engage every day, in their own style or way … Every parent, regardless of culture, language or experience, has something to offer. Even parents who feel they lack the skills or confidence to support the curriculum, can stress the value of education and be strong role models of learning.

To ensure that schools across the world embed parental engagement effectively, GEMS has also developed a set of standards against which schools can measure their progress.

GEMS is increasingly using action research as the means by which teachers reflect on their work with parents. It is also beginning to explore the ways in which parents can actively support the development of certain key dispositions such as international mindedness.

••

Stories from the frontline of expansive education: developing the culture and practices of enquiring teachers

The last of our four meanings of expansive education focuses on what expansive professional development predicated on teacher enquiry looks like. We have already touched on some of the underpinning evidence for the value of action research and for professional learning communities in Chapter 2. A number of the organisations and initiatives whose stories we told in this chapter are explicitly using enquiry as a means of evaluating practice and sharing knowledge:

▶ Bankstown Girls' High School has created a Community of Practice and Enquiry to develop its own expansive practices
▶ Expansive Learning Network has action research as one of its preferred methods
▶ The RSA Academy has been undertaking action research into the operation of the RSA Opening Minds curriculum as part of its membership of the Expansive Education Network[91]
▶ The Expansive Education Network is itself predicated on a professional network of teachers undertaking their own enquiries.

Another founding pioneer member of the Expansive Education Network, the Centre for the Use of Research and Evidence in Education (CUREE), is an example of a research-based organisation providing professional development and supporting teachers in developing their own research into expansive education.

Example: CUREE

CUREE is an internationally acknowledged centre of expertise in evidence-based practice in all sectors of education exploring teaching, research, communications and knowledge management. CUREE works with and for schools and colleges, academy chains, teaching schools and other clusters and alliances, professional associations, universities and government departments and agencies in the United Kingdom and beyond.

All CUREE's work is rooted in evidence and designed to help teachers make informed decisions about the most effective and efficient approaches to use in their own context. CUREE undertakes systematic research and reviews to find research that will be of most use to practitioners, and, using evidence about effective learning processes, creates accessible tools for professional development, for teaching and learning and for organisational development.

CUREE runs professional development on many aspects of expansive education including the development of growth mindsets for all and the encouragement of collaborative learning.

CUREE told us that their association with expansive education was for three reasons:

1. the evidence that an expansive approach is associated with improved outcomes for children
2. an appreciation that taking more expansive approaches to professional development will build staff capacity
3. the belief that it is a moral imperative—an expansive approach will equip young people to fulfil their potential.

CUREE works closely with expansive education pioneer, RSA Opening Minds.

Where CUREE is strongly expansive in its adoption of and support for teacher research, other organisations espousing action research in the United Kingdom and across the world tend to be broader in their scope. The following examples offer a flavour of this kind of practitioner enquiry:

▶ Many university departments support or encourage action research as part of Master's level work or as part of their work with teachers, for example, Jack Whitehead's living educational theory approach at Liverpool Hope University.[92]
▶ The independent research charity NfER coordinates a teacher network of action researchers in the United Kingdom and has published these results as well as evidence of benefits to schools.[93]
▶ The commitment by the Association of Chartered Teachers in Scotland[94] to reflective practice and teacher enquiry.
▶ The Action Learning, Action Research Association (ALARA)[95] in Australia, which brings together a network of people interested in using action research and action learning to generate collaborative

learning, research and action to transform workplaces, schools, colleges, universities, communities, voluntary organisations, governments and businesses.

▶ The Action Research Network in Alberta (ARNIA)[96], which coordinates activities for teachers and publishes support materials.[97]

The proof of concept—that teachers are ready, willing and able, with support, to undertake their own action research—has been well-made. What is much more tentative is getting teachers who believe in and are undertaking expansive approaches to also undertake action research and so build up the practitioner evidence-base.

In a small way, the Centre for Real-World Learning has supported this kind of work in Cardiff, Milton Keynes and Ealing, by working with teachers who specifically want to frame their enquiries expansively. Most recently, we have established an action research group exploring aspects of Building Learning with the not-for-profit organisation, Teaching Leaders. Under the aegis of the Expansive Education Network in England and Wales, we have been working with a partnership of ten universities to design and deliver action research training to teachers and then to guide them through the process. The outputs of this are published on the Expansive Education Network site in the member area.

The focus of the enquiries of teachers we are collectively working with shifts away from traditional interest in aspects of subject knowledge, delivery or organisational structures towards best ways of developing dispositions, the practical implications of growth mindsets or an understanding of which dispositions for learning are well developed when out-of-school locations are used.

Using the standard action research question frame of 'If I do "x", will "y" happen?', more expansive questions are created, such as:

▶ If I stop answering the questions of my Year 10 students, will they become more resilient?

▶ If Year 7 students have to teach Year 3 pupils to read, will Year 7 become more confident readers?

▶ If Year 8 students critique each other's Design and Technology projects, will their reflectiveness improve?

▶ If Year 4 pupils take on the role of question detectives, will they ask better questions?

▶ If Year 6 students mark each other's maths, will the markers' understanding of maths improve?

▶ If I encourage my pupils to develop growth mindsets, will their resilience improve?

▶ If I encourage Year 12 students to visualise chemical reactions, will this help them understand the concepts?

▶ If I coach my pupils in adopting different perspectives in history, will that transfer to the playground?

▶ If I provide opportunities for extended project work, will this develop more reflectiveness in Year 8 art students?

▶ If I encourage pupils actively to monitor their levels of concentration, will their absorption improve?

▶ If students identify and undertake one new or different risk a week, will it increase their ability to seek and embrace new experiences?

▶ If I provide maths games for parents to use at home, will their children's confidence in maths increase?

One school in England has taken the idea of action research so seriously that it has started its own action research journal.

School case study: Bay House School

Bay House School is an 11–18 comprehensive state school in Gosport, England with more than 2000 students on its roll. Under the leadership of its head teacher, Ian Potter, it has taken a number of the approaches described in this chapter—BLP, Personal, Learning and Thinking Skills, Carol Dweck's growth mindset thinking and ideas of professional learning communities—and created its own unique blend of approaches. Ofsted inspectors recently rated the school as outstanding and relayed a telling parent's comment in their report's opening paragraph:

> As a result of the teachers' belief in a teenager, my child has grown enormously emotionally and intellectually to prove them right.[98]

At Bay House, all teachers are encouraged to undertake enquiries and participate in learning communities. This, rather than more traditional in-service training, has become the main focus for the school's professional development. Every term, it publishes the *Bay House and GEIP Journal of Educational Research*.[99] Topics recently explored include: teachers as role models, philosophy for children, growth mindsets and positivist versus interpretivist views of the world. The December 2012 edition of the journal carries an interview with Dr Chris Watkins from London University's Institute for Education, exploring the creation of classroom learning communities and one from Dr Alison Taysum of the University of Leicester, who explores the importance of encouraging a spirit of enquiry in schools. This edition also carries a feature on learning beyond the classroom which explores the shift in language from 'home work' to 'home learning' and how Bay House is seeking to set home learning tasks which embody the '3Cs' of 'choice', 'challenge' and 'creativity'.

Bay House explicitly refers to its teachers as learners. Professional development for the staff is much more about ongoing enquiry and learning communities than traditional training. The school is a member of the Expansive Education Network and Ian Potter has been a powerful advocate for the importance of the research function in schools as a means of improving the quality of teaching and learning. He believes in developing further the construct of reflective practitioner so that teachers and supporting staff perceive themselves as 'researching professionals', and he pushes for links with the higher education sector in order to facilitate dialogue between his school and 'professional researchers'. Thus, his strategy for deepening the professional reflection within Bay House is to encourage engagement between academics and practitioners.

We have also been working closely with two internationally well-known private schools, Eton College and Wellington College, both of which, in different ways, strongly and publicly endorse expansive education. Eton College explicitly seeks to develop certain dispositions in its students:

> ... *most importantly the 'arts and habits' that last for a lifetime. Our primary aim is to encourage each Etonian to be a self-confident, inquiring, tolerant, positive young man, a well-rounded character with an independent mind, an individual who respects the differences of others.*[100]

Eton has recently introduced action research to its staff as key element of its professional development.

Wellington College runs an annual conference every summer at which many of the approaches we have included in this book are showcased, as well as championing its 'eight aptitude' approach, based on the work of Howard Gardner (see pages 33 and 34) to cultivate certain core attributes.

There is growing interest in these approaches, too, from educational institutions dealing in post-16 teaching. Oxford and Cherwell Valley College (OCVC) in England is a good example of an institution that has embraced the spirit of expansive education. Increasingly, teaching at OCVC is organised around Learning Zones, deliberately seeking to integrate different disciplines, and it is becoming normal for older students to be actively involved in teaching, for example, by organising conferences for their younger peers. OCVC's learning manager gave us a clear sense of where colleges like hers are trying to move:

> *In FE [post-16 education] we seem to only play the qualification game and pay far too little attention to growing our young people's*

brains around enabling them to learn how they learn. If we are to engage young people we have to learn to play the other game; that is to pick up on their motivations, enthusiasm, curiosity and start noticing the motivations with which they have arrived; encourage project based learning not just outcomes and assessments. We need to encourage collaborative cross discipline working, new curriculum models and encourage learning beyond the 4 walls, so learners 'flow' and 'flourish'. We need to encourage creative ways of working and incubate ideas and entrepreneurship that will lead to employment, particularly in vocational settings.

Throughout the book, we have stressed that there is a strong association between what teachers believe to be good for their students and what they believe (and do) in their own professional lives. One school in Singapore has begun to explore this connection explicitly.

School case study: The Australian International School

The Australian International School (AIS) is an International Baccalaureate Organisation (IBO) World School based in Singapore that was first established in 1993. The school is home to over 2700 students and 300 teaching staff, with more than 45 different nationalities represented within the community. AIS caters for students aged from 3 to 18—from preschool through to the conclusion of their secondary schooling. As part of an expansive approach to education, the school aims to provide an outstanding academic environment, while also supporting students to develop the personal qualities, thinking skills and effective learning dispositions that will enable them to be successful in their future lives and learning.

What distinguishes the school is that its vision for expansive education is inclusive of all members of the school community—students, teachers, school leaders and parents. AIS aims to provide a dynamic and nurturing learning environment for all of these key stakeholders; as a way of acknowledging the interdependent nature of their relationship within a school setting and the power they have to inform each other's learning. The principal method being employed within the school to promote this educational vision is collaborative inquiry. From the Executive Boardroom to the preschool classroom, from a professional learning workshop to a meeting of the Parents' Association, all members of the school community are engaged in inquiry-based learning, as a vehicle for their own learning and as a way of contributing towards the mission of the school.

Collaborative inquiry at AIS is seen as not only the most effective way of working together to support collective learning, but also as a way of building and sustaining a thoughtful learning culture in the school. Whether it is through the influence of Reggio Emilia¶ in a preschool classroom or through use of the tools for systems thinking in senior leadership forums, the thoughtfulness of the school culture is a tangible presence. In many ways, the most important and difficult challenge facing the school is to preserve and further develop this positive learning culture in the always dynamic, and often turbulent, environment of international education.

A critical structure used within the school for this end is an approach to professional learning that is focused upon collaborative teacher inquiry. Each year, all members of the teaching staff are involved in a Teacher Inquiry Group (TIG) program over the course of a semester. The main learning focus for the program is the exploration and promotion of 21st century skills; with teachers inquiring into student learning and classroom practice in areas such as digital literacy, collaboration, knowledge building, effective learning dispositions and critical thinking. The program has grown over the course of three years from an initial trial in the Primary School to become part of a whole-school platform for professional learning.

The TIG program developed at AIS has a solid grounding in core concepts and practices associated with action research. While there is considerable diversity in the way each group of teachers conducts their inquiries, an initial and enduring focus for the work of each TIG is the development of shared approaches to planning, the collection and analysis of data, reflection on practice and the determination of future action. Elements of choice are built into the program, with teachers able to select an area of focus for their inquiries, while group facilitators are also drawn from a pool of staff volunteers with

¶ A world-famous approach to early years education started by Loris Malaguzzi, who was a teacher, and which also involved the parents in the villages around Reggio Emilia in Italy after World War II.

particular expertise in a given field. While teachers play a vital role in the selection of various lines of inquiry, important guidelines for the work of each group include direct alignment with the school strategic goals in the area of 21st century learning, along a rigorous commitment to the exploration of everyday teaching practice and student learning.

Each year, the school conducts research into the operation, impact and effectiveness of the TIG program, in line with the following guiding question: How can we develop sustainable systems that promote ongoing improvement in professional learning, student learning and strategic school development? Findings to date have shown that the program is having a transformative effect on the school's learning culture.

Through the TIG program, teachers at AIS report that they feel supported to experiment with and explore their practice in relation to the incorporation of a focus on 21st century skills. Significantly, they also describe the high-level impact that their learning has had on their classroom practice and the learning of the students in their classrooms. The studies conducted to date have highlighted the power of developing structures and systems that align the learning of students, teachers and school leaders, with the goal of developing a school-wide culture of inquiry and learning as relevant and vital for the adult learners, as it is for the students.

There are a number of exciting next steps planned for expansive education at AIS. In relation to the TIG model, there will be an increased focus on the use of data to examine the impact of the program on student learning, including an emphasis on the study of qualitative data to investigate the development of effective learning dispositions in relation to 21st century skills by the students. At a whole-school level, the school plans to explore further how to genuinely engage parents as members of the learning community through the development of forums that support their learning, while also drawing on their experience and knowledge to improve the educational programs offered by the school. In the next year, one of the biggest projects being undertaken by the school is the implementation of a whole-school system for professional learning and review. Based on principles of Stewardship, the system is designed to incorporate the school's approaches to teacher inquiry, classroom observation and coaching within an integrated structure that supports ongoing organisational growth.

This story is increasingly being replicated the world over. Whether working in privately or publicly funded education, a growing number of educators are seeing that expansive approaches are in tune with the kinds of schools we need to create if we are to educate learners for the real world, which is itself an uncertain and changing place. So we find the Center for the Future of Elementary Education at Curtis School in Los Angeles[101] promoting to private schools ideas of the kind we described as emanating from Sir Ken Robinson on page 38 and from P21 on page 62. Expansive education knows no country or class boundaries. Children are children wherever they are and whoever is paying.

The impacts of expansive education

This book has not been written as a formal evaluation of the impact of expansive education, although wherever we have found reliable evaluation or research on aspects of our pioneers' work, we have cited it. Such a systematic job of research will soon need to be done, and we hope that it will be. Nevertheless, we will take a moment here to comment informally on the kinds of impacts we are noticing on curricula, on teachers, on the wider educational community and, ultimately, on learners themselves.

Clearly, there are considerable direct impacts on learners through the organisation of the curriculum, such as by developing a competence- or project-based approach to curriculum, or by promoting a particular approach to how cross-curricular teaching is conducted. The Leonardo Effect takes an interdisciplinary approach to teaching and learning, which places art and science equally at the core. Its approach to cross-curricular teaching aims to provide deep, coherent connections that facilitate development of learning dispositions. DaVinci Academy has a 'learn-by-doing' model, integrating core subjects with real-life problem solving and involving families as facilitators. Wellington College's Year 9 pupils study the International Baccalaureate Middle Years Programme, in which learning competencies are explicitly written into the syllabus. The Curriculum Foundation provides a curriculum model enabling schools to link broad competencies to subject areas within a unified approach. The RSA Academy was set up to develop the competence-based approach to learning. All of these models have profound implications on pedagogy, which we explore in Chapter 4.

Another way organisations impact directly upon learners is to provide some form of training. This could be aimed at teachers, at learners or at parents. Specialist training takes an expansive focus when, for example, it looks at how to develop critical thinking in learners, or how best to learn based on the latest cognitive advances. Many of the specific approaches described in this chapter have their own training arm. But perhaps the more profound shift is a move away from a reliance on external training, to a recognition that teachers are actors in their own classroom dramas and that approaches such as action research can help them become more precise in their reflections on the impact of their daily instructional decisions on pupils.

Some organisations work to develop partnerships, perhaps with parents, or with the community and businesses. Still others provide resources such as schemes of work, curriculum resources or training materials. Finally, organisations may work to develop a particular teacher activity. This may be discussion and space for reflection. Alternatively, it may be to promote the researching of teachers' own professional practice through such means as action research.

Many expansive organisations provide external recognition or validation of the work in schools. The Thinking Schools, for example, accredit organisations that are using their approach. Others, like ASDAN, develop qualifications that take account of the values of expansive education. Some organisations, like CUREE, conduct or promote research that supports their approach to education, and still others create publications that reach a wider audience. Most pioneers are running either formal or informal membership schemes or communities of practice to facilitate constructive dialogue among educators.

Many organisations provide consultancy services, conducted with a view to developing certain practices and often funding not-for-profit advocacy work, too.

Sadly, we found almost no evidence that new thinking is impacting on initial teacher education.

Some expansive voices

In the course of our research, we received many profound and thoughtful responses, a few of which we reproduce here by way of rounding off this chapter.

A recurrent theme was the failure of much educational provision to serve the needs of young people. Another was rapid rate of change in the world and schools' failure to keep up with it.

A quotation from a Project Leader at Learning Futures illustrates the first issue:

> *There are many third-sector organisations, and schools who have swum against the tide of government-induced compliance and fear. They struggle to come together to present a coherent argument for an education system which seeks to prepare young people with the knowledge and skills which will be needed in an entrepreneurial future. Expansive is a good word, but should not just apply to breadth of approaches. We have to expand the minds of parents and students to see that an overly narrow focus on examination results, and Ofsted approval is not serving the long-term prospects of our young people. Increasing numbers of young*

people are struggling to adapt to the habits of mind needed for higher education and the world of work.

Words from the Founding Principal of the DaVinci Academy in Los Angeles illustrate the second concern. In a fast-changing world where the role of education now lies in expanding learners' capacities to develop the learning dispositions and skills they need in order to engage effectively with new and complex situations:

Teaching learners for the real world involves the recognition that the world is changing, and the acceptance that we may not know what it will look like in terms of career opportunities and avenues for our students. An expansion of our pedagogy is imperative to prepare learners for an uncertain world: while subject-specific content knowledge and applications may be just as pertinent today as ever before, it is more important now than ever to instill in our learners the capacity to own and be in charge of their learning.

By enabling ongoing dialogue between teachers and pupils, SAPERE's approach fosters more thoughtful, constructive teacher responses to pupils' ideas, which, in turn, encourages pupils to develop further their own reasoning and questioning. The classroom thus becomes the place in which all members reflect more deeply on conduct, concepts, knowledge, attitudes and values.

The Leonardo Effect suggests that expansive approaches to teaching and learning enable teachers to find their role more fulfilling as they engage in learning with pupils rather than simply teaching *at* pupils.

Another strand of comments centred on the desirability of teachers becoming learners. A teacher whose own views truly align with an expansive mindset has already made a commitment to learning. DaVinci Academy's Founder again puts her finger on this well:

In order to teach expansively, we must expand our own capacities as learners. As immigrants in the new world of technology, research and creative educational opportunity, we must embark on this journey into a new world with eyes wide open: in learning how to use the essential tools available to us today, we acquire skills to operate efficiently within a range of complex systems.

Through the first tentative steps towards engaging in expansive education—particularly through beginning to understand how learning happens—teachers can begin to view learners and the learning process in a new way. As QED's Director of Learning Platforms says:

Leaders and educators alike see the value in better understanding the neurological workings of the mind. Many find that in the process of learning about it, they learn to see students as well as themselves differently. A subtle shift in one's thinking about learning through strengths can pay huge dividends in the thousands of tiny interactions between teachers and students.

The work of CUREE, and of Mindset Works, aims in part to develop a growth mindset in practitioners as well as learners. As Mindset Works co-founder told us, 'In this way, educators become better able to support students as the students adopt growth mindset beliefs and develop metacognitive competencies'.

We end with a salutary reminder about the ease with which we can polarise complex discussions. As we have said throughout this book, expansive education is both about preparing learners for real life *and* preparing them for success in the examinations that they encounter along the educational highway. These two goals are not mutually exclusive and, in fact, the expansive approach is at the very core of successful learning. Here's Mindset Works co-founder again:

The expansive education approach is often misunderstood as a desire to teach students things that are not part of core learning. It is often seen as a luxury when human and financial resources are in short supply. It is important to convey that the expansive education approach is at the heart of learning.

Chapter 4

Expansive pedagogy: a new model

> *An expansion of our pedagogy is imperative to prepare learners for an uncertain world. While subject-specific content knowledge and applications may be just as pertinent today as ever before, it is more important now than ever to instill in our learners the capacity to own and be in charge of their learning.*
>
> Dr Nicole Tempel Assisi,
> Founding Principal, DaVinci Schools

This challenge from expansive education pioneer, Nicole Tempel Assisi, is the one we try to answer in this chapter. Exactly what is or might be different in terms of pedagogy if you are trying to teach expansively? How does your approach change if you are explicitly seeking to cultivate certain dispositions for life and learning? In what ways do methods need to change if your assumption is that intelligence is learnable and mindset really matters? How can teachers connect with the real world outside their classroom in a routine and sustainable way? And, if teachers are explicitly seeking to be learners engaged on a lifelong journey of enquiry too, how does this impact upon their pedagogical processes?

In short, we want to get closer to understanding more about the choices teachers and educators take on a moment-by-moment, lesson-by-lesson, daily, weekly, termly, course-based and long-term strategic basis. In doing this, we will specifically be drawing on research we have undertaken in the last five years[1], as well as on the thinking of many whom we have already cited in Chapters 2 and 3.

Defining pedagogy

The term pedagogy is not much used in the United Kingdom these days, though there have been signs recently that it is coming back into favour. In Europe, it is much more widely accepted and in the United States and some other English-speaking countries, the phrase 'instructional design' is often used as a close synonym for pedagogy, with 'instruction' carrying a broader meaning than the more didactic sense it has in the United Kingdom.

We start from a broad definition of pedagogy. Where once it meant little more than the way 'instruction' is undertaken in the classroom by the teacher, we see it having a much wider sense to include not just the implied didactic element but also the roles learners have in being active participants in the process. So, our working definition is:

Pedagogy is the science, art and craft of teaching and learning. It includes all of the decisions which are taken to create the broader learning culture in which teaching takes place, especially with regard to the purposes of education—the dispositions that are most valued, the beliefs about intelligence, the governing assumptions about where and how learning in school happens and the roles of teachers and learners in the process. Pedagogy is a set of decisions that teachers and course designers take to orchestrate teaching and learning to achieve their desired outcomes.

The decisions that shape the culture of a school or a space like a classroom or workshop have started to happen before the 'teacher' even enters. They have been taken either consciously or non-consciously by those who lead the institution and will be influencing many things such as the way adults talk to students, what is displayed on the walls and, very importantly, which things get noticed and rewarded and which are not valued or are discouraged. On this last score, decisions about the ways different kinds of assessment are used and talked about have a significant impact.

So, too, pedagogy does not stop at the lesson's end. Decisions about what, if any, homework is set and how it is used (or not), decisions about the degree to which families are or are not encouraged to be part of the learning process after the lesson has finished and the degree to which pupils' outside lives are recognised, prepared for and consciously learned from—all of these and more affect pedagogy in practice.

Implied in our definition is an answer to the question from which any discussion about pedagogy must begin: 'Pedagogy for what?' As the subtitle of this book indicates—*teaching learners for the real world*—we are clear about the outcomes we think we are seeking. We want students to emerge from the school system with the kinds of dispositions and mindsets that will enable them to thrive in an uncertain world. This means that the outcomes of effective expansive learning need, as a minimum, to include:

1. routine capability (the disposition and expertise to be ready, willing and able to use what has been learnt, often non-consciously, for specific situations)
2. non-routine capability (the resourcefulness to be able to stop and think and then use what has been learnt before in situations that are novel or difficult or where there is a lack of support)
3. an ethic of excellence (self-belief, a determination to learn from others and pride in learning activities well done)

4. wider dispositions for lifelong learning (a transferable set of learning tactics, heuristics and attitudes).

As we think about expansive pedagogy, we will want to bear in mind these four desired outcomes.

These outcomes are important as a counterweight to much of the published theoretical understanding of pedagogy, which has been drawn largely from the experience of teaching of academic subjects, *not* from an assumption that we are cultivating certain important habits of mind or capabilities. This literature can drag us down to take decisions that are more about instrumental accountability than expansive education. As a result, there can be an over-emphasis on decontextualised recall and regurgitation rather than on deep understanding, application and new thinking.

Now that we are clearer about desirable outcomes, we need to touch, briefly, on four more variables: teachers, learner, learning environments and teaching and learning methods.

Teachers, learners and expansive education

In expansive classrooms the relationship between teachers and learners is different from the one found in more traditional ones. Expansive learners do more and learn differently, and expansive teachers seem, on the surface, to be doing less and are certainly doing things differently.

But if this sounds like a charter for loosely structured progressive, student-centred education, nothing could be further from the truth. While of course students' needs and their voices are centrally important, the focus in expansive education is on the desired outcomes of developing young people's capabilities so that, as they go through school they acquire certain dispositions for learning and, when they leave school they are equipped to thrive at home, at work and in the wider community settings in which they will be living.

Teachers will be constantly asking and trying to answer a number of key questions:

1. How can I ensure that all learners develop growth mindsets?
2. How can I make activities as authentic and engaging as possible and at the same time expand the horizons of learners?
3. How can I make enquiry and questioning a central feature of all that we do?
4. How can I ensure that I offer learners the best blend of theoretical explanation and practical experience?
5. How can I create opportunities for learners to go deeper, become immersed and strive for excellence?
6. How can I organise classes in ways that actively encourage students to see themselves as part of a community or studio, making best use of all available resources?
7. How can I develop patterns of collaborative learning so that learners are well equipped to learn, play and work together with others and in a variety of contexts?
8. How do I ensure that the processes of learning are explicit and that the language we use to describe them is well understood by all?
9. How can I make best use of face-to-face time and harness the resources of the virtual world?
10. How can I best facilitate the development of all the learners in my class?

Each of these questions is complex and requires the best efforts of teachers, supported by deep understanding of the topics that each question explores. We have already touched on some of the science behind each of them and on pages 138 to 157 we explore each in turn, summarising some key lines of thinking.

John Hattie has very helpfully described the ways in which teacher mindset needs to change, to what he calls 'desirable mind frames', if teachers are to have maximum impact on student learning. Here, we paraphrase his thinking.

The teacher's main task is to notice the impact of their teaching on students' learning and achievement. Teachers need to think of themselves as change agents, changing students from where they are to what they can be. They are adaptive experts in learning, able to coach and model different ways of learning while actively seeking feedback about their impact on students.

Teachers need to talk less and listen more. Their job is constantly to be challenging and stretching learners, making their learning intentions and success criteria as explicit as possible, within climates that encourage them to share perceptions about their impact on students' learning. It is essential that teachers develop and share a common language of learning with students and parents alike.[2]

Hattie's description exactly applies to expansive teachers, whose focus is on visibility of learning processes (the development of powerful learning dispositions) and maximising student learning and achievement. Hattie's strongly evidenced arguments do not explicitly seek to create the kinds of expansive outcomes we have been arguing for in this book but his emphasis on teachers becoming better noticers of their own impact is very much allied.

In classrooms organised along expansive lines, the role of the learner inevitably changes dramatically. Two metaphors help to illustrate the essence of this shift. If schools were ships, learners would be on the bridge helping to plot a course rather than being either passengers sitting back and enjoying the trip or in the engine room waiting for the captain's command. If schools were theatres, they would be modern studio versions of the kind where there are no curtains, the audience is frequently part of the drama and the director is constantly inviting the audience to 'come backstage' to see what is going on.

Expansive education is for all students of whatever age. And, regardless of age, learners in expansive classrooms can expect to play many new roles. They can be the designer or co-designer of the lesson or part of it. They can act as peer teachers. They can be coaches to each other and mentors to younger or less skilled students. They can be 'inspectors', trained to give their teachers feedback in ways that are formatively useful and appropriately respectful. They can even be educational researchers undertaking not just curricular enquiries but also actively being recruited to understand more about the learning processes in which they are involved—for example, monitoring their own levels of focus or distractibility, trying out and evaluating different methods of learning the same content, or experimenting with different kinds of questioning techniques and noticing the results.

Expansive learning environments

We have already seen how much context and culture matters (see pages 19 to 22) and this is bound to be important in the classrooms, studios, workshops, laboratories and music rooms in which students learn. While the physical setting may be very different according to location in the world and age of child, there are two abiding characteristics of successful expansive learning environments. They are stretching and feedback rich.

By stretching, we mean that the way they are set out is designed to stretch all who learn there. At its simplest, this might be a poster with the question: 'How could you make what you have just done harder for yourself?' Or, using technology, it might be that it is easy for students who have completed a task at one level to quickly transfer their attentions to the next level up.

By feedback-rich, we mean that everything about the environment encourages critical reflection on progress. Here, a simple example might be a display of work in progress, helpfully annotated in another colour by both students and teacher alike with feedback comments for all to see and learn from.

Perhaps the most apt image for expansive classroom is of a 'mind gym'.** The exercise machines are subjects, topics and activities, and the fitness coaches who work in this space are helping learners to exercise not their physical but their mental 'muscles'.

Ron Ritchhart has a nice phrase to describe the kinds of places we are trying to conjure up. He calls them 'thoughtful environments'[3], and notes a number of important characteristics. Thoughtful environments encourage a focus on big ideas that are important to the subject being studied, thus making the investment of time and effort worthwhile. The learning offered in them captures the interest of students and provides them with some degree of autonomy and choice. And always in these places there is a teacher who is modelling his or her own interests in whichever disposition is being cultivated.

In expansive environments, one word needs to be used especially carefully: ability. This word can so easily slip into becoming a synonym for 'talent' or 'intelligence'. But worse still, as Carol Dweck's work on mindsets has made clear, the use of ability as a concept can become almost indistinguishable from a belief that ability is largely fixed. Even if the adverb 'currently' is used as a prefix to descriptions of progress such as 'currently less able' or, perhaps, more plausibly, 'currently achieving a level x in y', the force of the word 'ability' in a school environment is often used to prejudge future progress. Very few schools manage to create learning groupings that are genuinely fluid and regularly changed. Yet it is only when this happens that pupils

---

** Not to be confused with 'brain gym', a proprietary method of supposedly increasing the connectivity of the brain through physical exercises.

have any empirical sense that being placed in a set is anything other than a judgment on their prospects.

Let's go back to our ten questions for a moment and ponder how a learning environment might be organised to promote expansive education.

1. Growth mindsets—posters throughout the school of people who have had to struggle to succeed.
2. Authenticity—where vocational subjects are taught in an environment that is really like 'the real thing'.
3. Centrality of enquiry—walls in each classroom carry examples of questions to which the teacher does not know the answer.
4. Theory and practice—glass walls which enable expert students to be observed and teachers to make theoretical observations to help other learners without unnecessary interruptions.
5. Expanded time—rooms which allow students to meet together for short plenary sessions in relatively large numbers and then have many break-out spaces for learning to continue and explore topics at greater depth for longer chunks of time.
6. Using tools—spaces that encourage learners to move around to make use of tools as and when they need them and to critique each others' work in progress.
7. Group work—flexible arrangements of tables and chairs, along with small spaces, which allow different permutations of group size to work together easily and effectively.
8. Visible learning—displays and conversations that explicitly show the processes of learning.
9. Virtual world—access to high-quality web resources available before and after school hours.
10. Facilitated learning—well sign-posted opportunities throughout the school for independent learning, along with clear indications of where resources can be found to facilitate this.

A decision-making framework for expansive pedagogy

If you are still reading this far into the book we'd like to think that you must be at least partially persuaded by the some of the science, or have found something in our stories from expansive pioneers that speaks to you. We hope that you share at least some of our four broad aspirational outcomes for expansive education. If you do, we believe that the emerging evidence we and others are uncovering means that you are in good company. But let's suppose you are a teacher and wanting to change your practice to become more expansive. What do you do? In the rest of this chapter we explore the choices that all teachers face when they want to shift their practice in the directions we and our pioneering friends are suggesting.

We started this chapter by suggesting that pedagogy is essentially a set of decisions that teachers and course designers take to orchestrate teaching and learning to achieve their desired outcomes. We think there are ten key decisions that teachers have to take and we have expressed these as a series of continua in the figure below.

While it might be tempting to assume that one end of each line is right and the other wrong, or one end better than the other, this is rarely the case. Most of these decisions are much more subtle. Where you 'place' yourself on any one line will depend on:

▶ the resources available to you
▶ the learners you are teaching
▶ the knowledge content you are seeking to explore
▶ the dispositions you are seeking to cultivate
▶ your own confidence.

These are the elements which, taken together, make up the context of your teaching and learning.

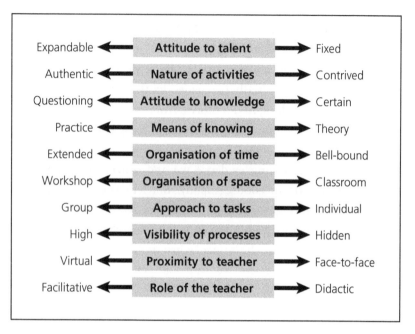

Figure 4.1 Ten choices for expansive educators

It is important to stress that this tool is not suggesting that these are binary, either–or decisions. Rather, the tool simply helps teachers to think about when one end of each of the choices may be more appropriate to adopt. Often it may be easier to plot a position somewhere along the continuum. So, for example, when a teacher is considering their own role, they will want to be thinking about which situations call for a more didactic approach and which will tend to be more effective if introduced in a more facilitative way.

Nevertheless, there has been a shift in thinking about pedagogic practice, which is moving broadly to the left of our figure and this is especially the case for those wishing to teach more expansively.

The diagram below indicates the kind of 'palette' from which teachers create their lessons and courses and the sort of approaches (colours) on which they tend to depend.

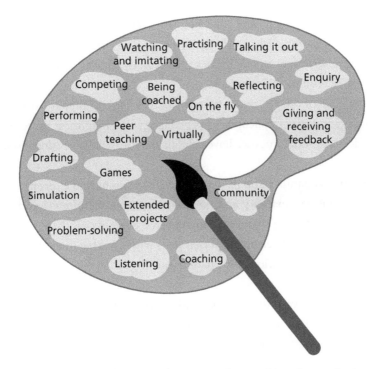

Figure 4.2 A palette of expansive teaching and learning methods

Unsurprisingly, expansive educators and their students tend to see it as part of their mission constantly to widen the range of possible learning methods, ensuring that learners have more choices as they go about their learning. Powerful learners can describe methods clearly to others and discuss the relative usefulness of different approaches and frequently they will not be using a single approach but be combining methods.

It is important to remember, too, that an understanding of methods is not sufficient in itself. For, it is often the way the method is used that is at least as important as the method itself. For example, we know of many schools adopting some kind of extended project. Some set this up in ways that are genuinely interdisciplinary, encouraging high levels of student engagement, empowering learners to plan their own routes through and building in well-planned critique and reflection sessions. Others use the same 'project' each year and leave very few genuine opportunities for collaboration, enquiry and personalisation to their students.

For each of our ten areas, we now try to bring together key lines of thinking, consider implications for pedagogy and map these on to the four desirable outcomes we have established for expansive education:

1. routine capability and its associated dispositions and expertise
2. non-routine capability and the necessary resourcefulness to adapt existing learning to novel or unexpected contexts
3. the pride and determination that goes with an ethic of excellence
4. the wider dispositions for lifelong learning.

Always we will want to be thinking about the degree to which choices can be made that genuinely prepare learners for the real world in which they will spend their lives (of which doing well at tests and examinations is only a part of a bigger picture). Sometimes we will want to focus on a particular method, such as, for example, the philosophical enquiry, which we described on page 96 or, more broadly, for example, on the set of practices often referred to as problem-based learning. On other occasions we will try to bring together the material to see to what extent we can make any useful generalisations about the choices that teachers make.

Attitude to talent: expandable or fixed

Whether you are successful or not in the real world depends to a large degree on how hard you have pushed yourself, how you have dealt with setbacks and how good you are at staying positive. Whether you possess these dispositions or not, as we have seen from Carol Dweck's research and from the results of the interventions led by Mindset Works (see page xx), is hugely influenced by the kind of learning mindset you have.

Those with a growth mindset see the making of mistakes as an indicator of effective learning. They enjoy stretching themselves and are always looking to see how they could be 'even better if ...', whereas those with fixed mindsets are more risk-averse and, wrongly thinking that their talent is innate, see little value in practising and putting in effort. They ascribe their success or failure in life (like their height or their eye colour) to their genes. Indeed, they can be effort-averse, believing that if you have ability you should not need to exert effort. In the real world, resilience is most often called for when the situation being encountered is either very difficult or more often simply non-routine and, therefore, novel.

There are a number of profound general pedagogic design principles that follow from this body of research. First, teachers talk to students in ways which transmit a belief in the learner's potential. Rather than reporting that student X has not mastered something, expansive teachers will prefer to say that student X has not 'yet' mastered it, unambiguously stressing the likelihood that they will do so. Even when something has been mastered, the assumption will always be that there is a next stage and a next stage to achieve.

But such stretching views of what is possible bring with them great challenges. So, secondly, the teacher seeks to provide support or scaffolding for learners to set ambitious goals but to receive appropriate support. Strategies abound for dealing with setbacks and building resilience. A BLP example of this is the 'stuck' poster, which students develop as an aide-mémoire for themselves to prompt a course of action when they get stuck. If you have ever watched the television program 'Who wants to be a millionaire', you'll recognise the kind of things that resilient learners do when momentarily stuck. They go 50–50, narrowing the odds. They phone a friend (the equivalent to using the internet as most 'friends' are simultaneously online). Or they ask the audience (like getting help with homework from your peer group at school).

Thirdly, expansive teachers who understand this core principle of growth see learning from mistakes as one of the most powerful tools in their pedagogic toolbox. Teachers invite learners to see constructive criticism as an important means of learning, not as something to be avoided out of embarrassment. They model how this might be done and give opportunities for simulation and role-playing. They admit to their own mistakes in life and what they have learned from them. They often share worked examples on the whiteboard, inviting group critical feedback.

Fourthly, teachers who see the power of growth mindsets may choose to offer a specific kind of support called 'deliberate practice[4].' Deliberate practice is good practising; practice that really helps you get better at something, whether you are learning a musical instrument, practising diving or using idiomatic French. Elsewhere, we have described five elements to this kind of practising[5]:

1. Getting the feel—over time, the body establishes a template of how it 'feels' when the action seems to be going well.
2. Automating—until 'muscle memory' has been established and the learner is able to execute the skills to the point when conscious thought is no longer required for each element of the action.
3. Picking out the hard parts—when an action does not lead to the desired outcome, the learner deconstructs that action to consider at which part the process went wrong.
4. Improvising—effective practice can involve a level of playfulness in trying new ways of working to avoid things becoming staid.
5. Doing it for real—skills become refined when they are tested in real-life situations, which may be competitive, stressful or pressured in some way.

There are many other ways of practising, widely used professionally in the arts and in sports from which teachers can learn.

Nature of activities: authentic or contrived

If your goal is to prepare learners for the real world, then schools may well cause you a problem, as the now famous description of school versus real-world learning by Lauren Resnick made clear on page 5. For, one of the major differences between schools and the world outside is the authenticity of the tasks that learners undertake.

In the real world, I learn about gas boilers when I need to buy one or mine has broken down, or about tree-planting because I need to screen an area from the sun or about good fiction writers for young people because I have an eight-year-old daughter. In such situations, I need immediate access to reference materials, to experts and to specialist expertise. My motivation is clear. I want to do something I can't do now. I am, in the broadest sense, trying to solve a problem.

Or it may be a more general or more complex issue I am addressing. I want to extend my circle of friends. I am worried about my health. I want to do something to help a family member who is going through difficult times. These examples are much messier and less well defined and will call for some preliminary sounding out, finding out, searching and thinking.

Schools are not much like either of these two sets of examples. Instead, their defining entry points tend to be the subjects which go to make up a school's timetable or curriculum. But schools could be a lot closer to life outside if they chose to be so!

David Perkins describes some of the tensions between the real world and the school world really helpfully in *Making learning whole*.[6] He makes a compelling case as to why and how schools can teach the whole game of learning (in other words, closer to the one we encounter in the real world). He puts his finger beautifully on two aberrations common in schools, which he calls 'elementitis' and 'aboutitis'. Both conspire to keep young people away from the world. Elementitis is the habit of breaking complex subjects up into meaningless chunks (learning the game of Scrabble, say, by listing from a dictionary four-letter words beginning with 'p'). Aboutitis is the tendency to teach *about* interesting ideas rather than seeing whether they work in practice. A good example of this was the way some teachers taught students about the idea of Howard Gardner's eight multiple intelligences and students then coloured in an imaginary profile of their strengths. Well-intentioned as this doubtless was, it did not help students to understand the deep and interesting ideas behind the theory but rather assumed that such aspects of intelligence were, like IQ, largely fixed.

Perkins offers us seven principles of whole-game learning, of which we quote the first two:

1. Play the whole game—use extended projects and authentic contexts.
2. Make the game worth playing—work hard at engaging learners giving them choices wherever possible.[7]

Methods that clearly fall into these two categories include: watching, imitating, enquiry, problem-solving, extended project work, competing and performing, although even these can intentionally or unintentionally be subverted to come across as contrived in the wrong hands!

Attitude to knowledge: questioning or certain

In much school learning, questions are asked and answers are given. There is often one correct answer. But as we get older and live our lives we realise that the really interesting issues in life often have many interpretations. Take the underlying question in this book about the purpose of school. There are many possible standpoints and ours is just one interpretation or approach.

Yet even when the subject is complex and interesting, teachers often speak with a certainty that brooks no challenge or leaves no room for subtlety. Why is this? Are we learning at an early period of our professional formation that teachers are always right? Are we afraid that an admission of not-knowingness would be a badge of shame?

In Chapter 2, we encountered Ellen Langer's research, which is pivotal here. Langer uses the concept of mindfulness to describe rich facilitative learning environments of the kind we are seeking to create in studio learning: 'A mindful approach to any activity has three characteristics: the continuous creation of new categories; openness to new information; and an implicit awareness of more than one perspective'.[8]

Langer has shown that small shifts in a teacher's language can induce a marked change in the learning habits that students are bringing to bear on their work. Specifically, if a teacher says definitively that something *is* the case, students take it literally and try to remember it. But if a teacher says, of the same thing, that it *could be* the case, they become more engaged, more thoughtful, more imaginative and more critical. 'Could be' language invites learners to become more active, inquisitive members of the knowledge-checking, knowledge-developing community, rather than to see themselves as 'merely' doing their best to understand and remember something that is already cut and dried.

David Perkins and colleagues go further still, arguing that: 'conditional instruction opens up possibilities, whereas absolute instruction tends to produce a more rigid mindset about the information'.[9] In this way, the teacher contributes to a mindful disposition and intelligent behaviour. Such tentative language suggests a more facilitative approach, one that invites multiple opinions, creates compelling environments in which learners can explore complex issues and in which it is frequently impossible to answer learners' questions definitively. It assumes that there will be many answers to most questions.

Of course there are many occasions when certainty is smart. When life is endangered. When dealing with some aspects of morality. When multiplying in base 10 and expecting that 2×2 will equal 4 and so on. But in the humanities, in the arts and when dealing with literature, multiple perspectives are to be expected. And there are questions of science and mathematics where we are still seeking answers and have only theories to offer at this stage.

Methods that encourage talking things out, enquiry, listening, drafting and giving and receiving feedback are likely to be sympathetic to a view of knowledge that assumes there will, on many occasions, be several different answers.

Means of knowing: practice or theory

In Chapter 2, we mentioned David Kolb as the researcher credited with the creation of the experiential cycle. We learn, he suggests, in a cycle that moves from concrete experience through reflective observation and abstract conceptualisation to active experimentation. And he is right for some situations. A child touches a hot log in an open fire for the first time and observes and reflects with a cry of pain. Later, she speculates that the burning part is, perhaps, part of a dragon or, like blood in stories, not necessarily a nice thing. She may go on to experiment and find out whether all wood in fires is painfully hot or she may have reached a compelling abstract theory that fire causes heat and wood burns and that wood in fires is to be avoided. Or maybe the child never touches burning wood because she has earlier had the idea of fire and heat explained so persuasively that she does not need to try it out for herself. Even in this relatively simple example it is becoming clear that there is no universally reliable experiential learning cycle! When one requires theory and when first-hand experience is better is a complex matter, depending on what is being learned, levels of experience, available resources and the broader context.

In expansive education, it is almost always the case that teachers will be using a blend of practical methods such as imitating, practising, sketching, problem-solving and extended project work as well as those that are more theoretical. Nevertheless, there is a presumption for expansive educators that, where possible, experiential opportunities will be sought with theory being offered as and when needed. Too often, theory is offered in chunks that are too big and too separate from practice, rather than, say, just before learning something, during the process of learning it via feedback or after the learning is completed, through reflective conversations.

Having a theoretical understanding is an essential part of the development of more complex learning outcomes such as the ability to deal with non-routine situations or the transfer of learning from one context to another. In both these examples, learners need to be able to see patterns, models and connections in order to be able to access something learned in the past. We know, for example, from the work of David Perkins and Gavriel Salomon that transfer is assisted by:

- extensive practice in different contexts
- specifically encouraging learners to consider how they might use what they are learning in other contexts at the point when they first learn something
- making as many connections as possible to the learner's existing knowledge
- the provision of clear models, explanations and mental models at the point of first learning a new skill.[10]

Extensive practice in different contexts helps to develop resourcefulness so that, to use a sporting metaphor, when a team plays away from home it is not thrown by the unfamiliarity of the ground. Specifically, considering other possible uses of something you are learning when you first learn invites you to really think what kind of thing it is you are learning and often moves it out of the domain of a subject to become a useful disposition.

So, back to the sports field for a moment; developing strategies for not getting upset when the opposing team scores a goal is a form of emotional self-management which, seen as such, is pretty similar to what you may have to do when you get stuck on a difficult maths question in a test. Connecting to the prior experiences of learners helps to ensure that their engagement is higher and that they are already being able to see, abstractly, that what they are learning is something like something else they know. And all of this is facilitated by the possession of mental models and rules that assist both transfer and more unconscious recall in less familiar situations. (What was it that helps when things suddenly go wrong? Ah yes, some way of delaying my response to give me some breathing space. I'll hold my breath and count to ten.)

Organisation of time: extended or bell-bound

The unit of work in the real world is a day, not an hour-long lesson, and almost every teacher we know will admit to the frustration of the bell going just when things are getting interesting. It takes time to become immersed in learning and to go deeper. Indeed, some of our pioneers in Chapter 3 have made this a cornerstone of their educational philosophy, so important do they consider this aspect of expansive teaching to be.

Something happens to the quality of our engagement engendered when we are engrossed in learning for an extended period of time. Mihaly Csikszentmihalyi has studied this phenomenon extensively and coined the word 'flow' to describe the state of mind that learners can achieve if they are deeply absorbed in their learning. He describes this as an optimal experience in which learners find deep fulfilment and in which they become unaware of time.[11] To achieve the state of flow, three things need to be in place: the task needs to be sufficiently demanding and engaging, the learner needs to have enough skill to be able to tackle the task without undue anxiety or stress and there needs to be sufficient time available.

There is clear evidence from Csikszentmihalyi's research that the quality of creativity increases when we are in a state of flow and that the experience of flow is itself inherently beneficial to the learner, who finds such experiences enjoyable and rewarding. Experiences like this do not come easily or when an individual is consciously relaxing. Rather, they involve, to use Csikszentmihalyi's own words, 'painful, risky, difficult activities that stretched the person's capacity and involved an element of novelty and discovery'.[12]

The state of flow is not unlike Ellen Langer's concept of mindfulness, in the sense that certain qualities of mind—effortless focus and absorption—are being cultivated. And, in terms of our conception of expansive learning and decisions about the organisation of time, we hypothesise that such deeper learning states are much more likely to occur within longer time frames. There are undoubtedly other potential benefits for learners of extended work. After extensive research into creativity, Lars Lindström[13] suggests, for example, that the disposition of creativity is fostered through investigative work that develops when students have opportunities to work on an assignment over an extended period of time.

In Lois Hetland's work on studio learning at Project Zero[14], projects often extended over a whole day and were carried out over a period of weeks. She links such extended periods of learning with increased engagement and persistence in learners. In most busy schools, the norm is for constant bell-induced interruptions. Yet a picture of expansive learning is already emerging of constructivist, authentic learning, which demands that problems be teased out by learners over more time than is typically allowed.

Extended projects clearly help, as do ways of engaging with learners outside the school and the school day, encouraging their activities to spill out beyond the end of classes and beyond the school gates into their homes and into the community. Different curriculum design is often called for and many of the competence-based pioneers mentioned in Chapter 3 have adopted timetables that facilitate learning in larger blocks of time. But even where such structural changes are not possible, teachers with an expansive mindset can help to transcend the compartmentalisation of the curriculum by explicitly expanding horizons and always suggesting ways in which connections can be made.

Organisation of space: workshop or classroom

We have already made some general observations about how spaces can promote expansive thinking. So, for example, if tools are locked away in cupboards it suggests that tools are controlled by the teacher rather than freely accessible. If dictionaries are stored on high shelves, it implies that pupils must ask the teacher before using one. If work in progress can be left out safely, then it might suggest that this interim stage of design was seen as a useful part of the process of making something. If drawers and cupboards are clearly labelled it might be assumed that students are encouraged to be resourceful and explore and use their contents. And so on.

We surmise that, just as one of the defining characteristics of *Homo sapiens* is our ability to create new tools, so one of the most important aspects of real-world learning is the ability to see what any new environment affords in terms of tools and human resources and then use them to best effect. Consequently, we imagine that a workshop environment is more likely to encourage exploration, experimentation, tinkering, prototyping and so on.

Teachers use space to underscore their learning intentions and personal belief sets. In characterising the physical organisation of space for expansive learning, we hope to make clear that the kinds of learning dispositions we are intending to cultivate are the kinds we have been exploring throughout this book. We should, as Roy Pea suggests, 'reorient the educational emphasis from individual, tool-free cognition to facilitating individuals' responsive and novel uses of resources for creative and intelligent activity alone and in collaboration'.[15]

Learning methods that are obviously workshop-based include watching, imitating, practising, drafting, sketching, conversation, reflecting—the kinds of things that happen naturally when a group of makers or artists are working in the same space and are curious to see how each other's endeavours are progressing.

Of central importance in thinking about expansive pedagogy is the desirability of providing opportunities for 'works in progress' to be stored, shown, seen and explored by other students. In an ideal world, teachers will choose to model their own creative or learning endeavours by sharing their works in progress too, either literally or through descriptions of their own learning.

Approach to tasks: group or individual

In the real world, teamwork is an essential way of working and learning. The ability to work collaboratively in groups to solve problems is one of the attributes cited by employers across the world as highly desirable. In almost all expansive curricula it is listed as a desired outcome of education.[16] Of course, we do not mean to suggest that individual learning is not valued; just that, in schools, individual performance tends to be emphasised rather than collaborative endeavour, certainly when it comes to assessment.

As we saw in Chapter 2, John Dewey argued strongly for a more cooperative approach to learning, variously using phrases like 'cooperative intelligence' and 'collective intelligence' a century ago. Dewey explained this by suggesting that for knowledge to be in any real sense useful it has to have expression in relationships and social activity. No man or woman is an island.[17]

As well as the social intelligence implied by watching and noticing others, there is a specific way that young people can help each other. Normally referred to as peer learning, this kind of group working occurs when learners explicitly seek to learn from and with each other. David Boud's description makes this clear: 'Students learn a great deal by explaining their ideas to others and by participating in activities in which they can learn from their peers'.[18]

Through the research of Jean Lave and Etienne Wenger[19], we have already seen in Chapter 2 how groups work and learn together. And as they work and solve problems together, so their learning habits and attitudes rub off on each other. New members watch carefully how the more established members talk, respond and deal with challenges, like children do when they want to join someone's 'gang'. This stage of 'legitimate peripheral participation' is an important element of expansive education.

Ikseon Choi and colleagues propose that peer interactions can guide and facilitate metacognitive activities, allowing existing knowledge to be reconstructed in their mind. In this way, peer interactions, particularly verbal interactions, have the potential to 'expand learners' awareness of what they need to learn'.[20] We saw earlier in this chapter some of the benefits of creating a classroom community of learners.

In terms of pedagogy, there is too often a lack of precision about exactly what is involved in any group process: what the roles to be played are, and how these will be developed and assessed. Group working provides the simplest way for us to learn by watching others.

A student watches the way one of her peers is starting to make a bird-box or paint a picture and tries to do it similarly. And teachers offer templates—techniques, tools, patterns of behaviour—for students to copy and make their own. Albert Bandura's work has explored the way we observe behaviour and its outcomes and then imitate (or avoid) what we observe. In Bandura's analysis we cannot escape the fact that we are all learning role models for each other. Bandura described the conditions necessary for effective imitation and modelling. First of all the learner must notice what is being modelled. Then she must remember and retain what has been noticed. And finally she must be able and willing to reproduce a desired behaviour. As Bandura nicely put it:

> *Learning would be exceedingly laborious, not to mention hazardous, if people had to rely solely on the effects of their own actions to inform them what to do. Fortunately, most human behaviour is learned observationally through modelling: from observing others one forms an idea of how new behaviours are performed, and on later occasions this coded information serves as a guide for action.*[21]

There are a number of approaches to group working used in schools that expansive educators may wish to explore, of which these are two kinds:

▶ The Group Investigation method emphasises a system of small groups, design of tasks requiring participation of each member, cooperation to accomplish its goals, synthesis of member contributions and an end presentation. Jigsaw learning is a good example in this tradition.[22]
▶ de Bono's '6 Thinking Hats'[23] is a widely used example and illustrative of the way in which by clearly delineating roles within groups, certain patterns of thinking and acting can be encouraged.

In the digital age, schools are also beginning to consider how best to create opportunities for online group working that is educational and safe (see later in this chapter on pages 153 to 154). Out of school it is clear to see, for example, the high levels of engagement engendered in online games played by young people who are connected to other players in real time across the world.

A begged question in most education systems is the issue of group assessment. Group work is hugely valued in life but at school there is a feeling that it is somehow not fair, a form of cheating, even (How will I know who has done the real work?). But until such collective endeavour is assessed, it is likely to remain valued more on the sports pitch and in the concert hall than as an integral part of learning in classrooms.

Visibility of processes: high or hidden

Buildings used to hide their central heating ducts and lighting cables until the Pompidou Centre in Paris made a feature of them. Well-produced plays used to pride themselves in hiding all aspects of stagecraft from the audience. Now plays such as Michael Frayn's *Noises Off*[24] make drama out of those hidden activities. And teachers used to think that they should keep many of the processes and methods of learning hidden and focus on the content and subject at hand—until recently, that is. We have known for fifty years that understanding more about the processes of our learning, sometimes called metacognition or metalearning, was potentially a useful thing for learners to do. And in the last decade, study after study has made explicit connections between understanding the processes of learning and the development of successful learning dispositions (as well as higher achievement).

Robert Sternberg, creator of the concept of 'successful intelligence', has developed a theory that makes explicit the links between intelligence and metacognition. As he puts it, metacognition is the executive process that people use for 'figuring out how to do a particular task or set of tasks, and then making sure that the task or set of tasks is done correctly'.[25]

David Perkins has similarly homed in on this executive process, which is capable of turning a thought into an action or a skill into a disposition, with the phrase 'reflective intelligence'.[26] We need to be able to recognise when it is appropriate to deploy certain kinds of thinking skills—to be sensitive to the occasion.

The title of John Hattie's book *Visible learning*, already mentioned on several occasions, speaks for itself. And he is explicit about his central contention in its early pages:

> *It is critical that teaching and learning are visible. There is no deep secret called 'teaching and learning'; teaching and learning are visible in the classrooms of successful teachers and students ... What is most important is that the teaching is visible to the student and that the learning is visible to the teacher.*[27]

The more that learners see what is going on as they are learning it, the better they will be able to understand and apply it in different contexts. Methods that invite high visibility of processes and focus on the 'how' of learning include watching and imitating, coaching, reflection and feedback. But any topic can be taught in a way that takes the student inside the mind of the learner and makes their learning processes explicit.

Proximity to teacher: virtual or face-to-face

In today's networked world, most of us are connected via the internet and its many social networking sites to many others on many occasions during any typical day. Through such methods our horizons have undoubtedly been expanded.

Indeed, the internet is forcing us to rethink the way we use the 'face time' we have at school. Certainly in terms of pedagogy, the virtual environment is a relatively new context for learning and lends itself to different habits of mind. Students can stop and start a TED lecture more easily than they can their teacher! Searching for information in your own time and your own way is the norm on the web. Well-honed scepticism is essential to distinguish good and bad, reliable and unreliable sources of information on the internet, while the classroom teacher should (in a perfect world, at least) be unimpeachable. Through surfing it may be far easier to see patterns and connections than ever before. Visual imagery is everywhere: with Google Earth, even what were once two-dimensional maps now provide 360° photographs of places.

One innovation beginning to be used in vocational education is flipped teaching. Drawing on work by Eric Mazur, the 'flip' here is to assume that, with technology, much of the lecturing and instruction can be done outside the classroom and time at college or school can be focused on higher-order interactions between teacher and learner.[28] This kind of approach could be a significant element of a contemporary approach to developing an expansive pedagogy.

Online worlds also allow opportunities for simulation, game playing, trial and error, safe practising and, increasingly, peer teaching. A good example of the latter is the Khan Academy[29], a free online education platform created by Salman Khan from a small office in his home, which now has thousands of video lessons teaching a wide spectrum of subjects.

For two decades, education has argued about the benefits or otherwise of virtual learning, often producing strong advocates for and against it, sometimes contrasting it unfavourably with face-to-face models of teaching, sometimes promoting it to such a degree that it becomes mindless cutting and pasting. A real debate is now happening at last and may enable us to get under the skin of virtual learning. For, like 'real' learning, it is prone to many of the same issues. Simply using it does not make you a better teacher or a more expansive learner. It is how you use it that counts.

The questions virtual learning raises for expansive educators include:

How can I use the virtual world to help my students:

▶ develop the dispositions I want them to acquire?
▶ reinforce the beliefs they have about the expandability of their intelligence?
▶ access worlds beyond the school gates?

Role of the teacher: facilitative or didactic

From the moment teachers enter a room full of students they are faced with choices about the role they play. They can be strict or lenient, serious or jokey, distant or accessible, quiet or loud and so on. But the decision they make about their overall approach, whether it is mainly facilitative or largely didactic, really matters, because it says much about their approach to knowledge, to learning and to learners. While being facilitative or being didactic may appear at first to be a straight choice of style, in reality it is more complex than the choices we have just listed.

The idea of the teacher as facilitator is not new: it has been explicitly part of an approach to learning referred to as 'constructivist' for about a hundred years. From a constructivist perspective, learning is created by an interaction between people's ideas and their experiences with other people. The goal of any learning intervention is the generation of new knowledge in collaboration with others. Such an approach requires resourcefulness and group-working skills in large measure. The core principles of the constructivist approach have been usefully summarised by John Savery and Thomas Duffy[30] and include the creation of authentic tasks that are anchored to the real world, high levels of ownership by learners of the tasks they undertake, learning environments that support and challenge learners' thinking and opportunities for learners to select as they develop alternative ideas and strategies.

Thus far, you might assume research suggests that expansive teaching is always best when facilitative. Not so. There are those who challenge the constructivist approach. So, for example, Paul Kirschner and colleagues ask us to think more carefully about *when* teacher guidance rather than freer facilitative approaches are beneficial. They argue that the architecture of the brain, specifically the processes of long-term and working memory, sometimes demands clear instruction rather than endless problem-based approaches. To be expert problem-solvers, they remind us, we need plenty of experiences stored in long-term memory and we need to be able to access these.

Facilitative styles of enquiry or problem-based learning require more short-term memory capacity and may thus leave less capacity available for thinking and learning. Kirschner and colleagues conclude: 'Controlled experiments almost uniformly indicate that, when dealing with novel information, learners should be explicitly shown what to do and how to do it'.[31] But we need to be careful to balance the aim of learning correct answers and procedures with the goal of developing independent learning dispositions. There is an even more powerful argument for the value of some kinds of didactic teaching which most of us will have in our memory bank. Think not of a teacher holding forth but of a really persuasive expert teacher demonstrating a complex craft or skill. Couple this with the compelling narrative and explanation they might offer us of what is being done and why, and you have the essence of the expert/apprentice/novice tradition of instruction.

Many people can recall such electrifying learning moments from their own school lives. Providing the processes of learning are made visible then these kinds of teacherly expositions are a different kind of didacticism from what is sometimes referred to today as the 'sage on the stage' (a teacher talking for a long time at students). It is a kind of cognitive apprenticeship that sits very comfortably within studio learning. Lois Hetland and colleagues at Harvard's Project Zero describe clearly the value of what they call the 'demonstration lecture', 'a brief, visually rich lecture by the teacher to the class (or to a small group) that conveys information that students will use immediately'. Such moments of didacticism work, the Project Zero research suggests, because they are focused, efficient, visually engaging, of immediate relevance, short and connected to skills and concepts *already* introduced.[32]

And the flip side of a change in teacher roles is a concomitant shift in what learners do, for what they do really matters. They need to be able to teach themselves and others, be resourceful, set challenging goals, give and receive feedback and generally be part of a classroom learning community.

A new framework for learning?

As a school tries to become more expansive, there is a lot to think about. Classroom pedagogy has to change, and that means systems of support and accountability—new kinds of professional development—may need to be devised and monitored. Subjects may be blended into themes and topics, and the structure of the timetable may well change as a result. Parents may need to be brought onside, and digital technology configured so that its use genuinely supports more independent and collaborative learning. And so on.

As a result of a recent evaluation of a group of Building Learning Power schools,[33] Maryl Chambers and her colleagues at The Learning Organisation (TLO) have developed a multi-layered route-map, the Learning Quality Framework (LQF)[34], to help school leaders plan and keep track of the constituent changes that add up to a more expansive learning environment. We think it might be useful to other expansive educators if we say a little more about the structure of this tool here.

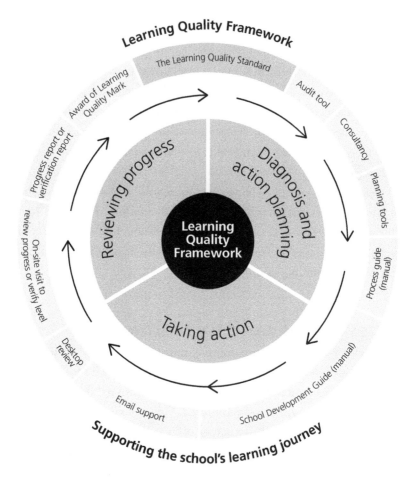

Figure 4.3 The Learning Quality Framework

The LQF describes twelve layers of change that contribute to moving a school in an expansive direction. They are:

1. **Vision for learning.** An engaging vision for 21st century education based on social, economic, moral and personal learning imperatives guides the development of the school and its community.

2. **A framework for learning.** A coherent approach to developing learning dispositions drives learning in the school and its community.

3. **A language for learning.** A rich language of learning permeates learning across the school and its community. The learning school develops, uses and extends a rich and dynamic language to talk about learning. Effective learning requires emotional engagement, a wide range of cognitive approaches, interpersonal interaction and personal responsibility. The language of learning that embraces all these dimensions is used to shape and improve learning in the school.

4. **Leading innovation in learning.** Leadership for learning throughout the school supports innovation, experimentation and risk-taking, building individual independence and responsibility in both staff and students.

5. **Professional development (PD) policy and strategy.** PD policy and strategy embraces a range of professional learning activities that stimulate and support communities of enquiry and research in the promotion of effective learning habits for all.

6. **Curriculum design.** The curriculum is effective in cultivating and progressing a set of generic learning habits and attitudes.

7. **Teaching methodology (pedagogy).** Learning opportunities intrigue and motivate learners, develop effective learning habits and enhance content acquisition.

8. **The learning environment.** The learning environment is used constructively to promote positive learning behaviours and reinforce messages about the nature of learning.

9. **Learner engagement.** Young people actively co-participate in the design, management and evaluation of learning and contribute to the powerful learning culture.

10. **Parents and community.** The school works in partnership with parents and carers to develop learning dispositions.

11. **Assessing for learning.** Tracking and authenticating the growth of learning dispositions (with regard to when, where and how well they are used) builds learners' motivation and informs learning design.
12. **Evaluating the learning organisation.** A monitored set of organisational learning indicators guides continual improvement in provision, practice and the achievement of objectives.

But it is not enough to have identified some of the facets of a school that can be recruited to support expansive culture change: you need to know what change in each of those layers actually looks like. How do you know how well you are doing already, in terms of recruiting parents' sympathy, for example? How is progress to be planned for, and recognised when it happens? The LQF offers a school leadership team a series of snapshots of what the next 'level' at each of the layers would look like, as well as a range of suggestions for activities that can help to move the school to the next level.

These are headlines only but they may serve to illustrate how the LQF offers a bigger context into which expansive pedagogy fits, and how useful it can be in supporting the journey towards providing a genuinely more expansive education. More information can be found on www.learningqualityframework.co.uk.

We leave the last words in this chapter to one of our pioneers, The Curriculum Foundation:

> Schools and nations do not have to choose between high standards within subjects, and an education that prepares young people for life. It is possible to have both. An expansive curriculum can excite imaginations, widen horizons, raise aspirations, inspire creativity, deepen subject understanding and can lay the roots of lifelong learning. It can send all young people out into the world with the confidence, the ability and the desire to make that world a better place.

Chapter 5

Expansive education: a theory and a call to action

The glue that binds the effective drivers [of change] together is the underlying attitude, philosophy, and theory of action. The mindset that works for the whole system reform is the one that inevitably generates individual and collective motivation and corresponding skills to transform the system.[1]

Michael Fullan

In this last chapter, we articulate our theory of action underpinning expansive education, and describe some of the barriers currently preventing expansive education from taking root on the ground. Then, we look briefly at what we know about how teachers most effectively change their habits. And finally, we summarise essential learnings from our own research into what seems to be working and bring this together into a call to action for all educators.

Our theory of action

The phrase 'theory of action' may not trip off the tongues of many teachers but we find it a helpful concept, encouraging as it does an explicit 'surfacing' of the beliefs and assumptions that sit beneath expansive education. Given that we have argued that action research is a core strategy for teachers, it also seems appropriate that we should frame our own expansive endeavours in similar vein.

Good questions in action research tend to look something like this:

If I do 'x', will 'y' happen?

Theories of action express their hypotheses not as a question but as a statement:

*If we do 'x' then 'y' **will** happen.*

Theories of action invite us to make our thinking explicit, to explain our rationale for choosing certain approaches rather than others and, drawing on evidence, to try and make a compelling case. Our theory of action, put simply, is:

> *If school systems across the world adopted the principles of expansive education, then young people would leave school as powerful learners, ready to thrive in a world of change as well as with the best possible examination results.*

So far, so straightforward. But any theory of action requires a theory of change, the means by which theory can become practice in the real world. To do this we need to focus on our *assumptions*, the *analysis* that sits beneath them and then the *actions* that flow from them.[2]

Assumptions

Our assumptions are that:

 in an uncertain and changing world, the goals of school must be broad, encompassing the development of the kinds of dispositions described throughout this book
 expansive education is complex (requiring teachers to see how the learning sciences are changing education and how new

understanding, for example with respect to learner mindset, can be put into practice)

▶ for many aspects of expansive education there is proof across the world that both the idea and its implementation are substantially do-able, even in those countries where schools are more restricted or constrained

▶ the broader definition of expansive education is emerging, organically, as a set of coherent approaches, which can be implemented increasingly coherently as our understanding continues to grow

▶ for expansive education to take root in classrooms, teachers have to take certain conscious decisions. These long-term, short-term and in-the-moment decisions, taken together with the culture and context of school, are what effectively create an expansive pedagogy

▶ changing teacher habits is hard! But we know at least some of the ingredients of successful habit change in teachers (such as cultures and practices of enquiry, pedagogic leadership and certain kinds of professional learning).

Analysis

The analysis that has led us to these assumptions is contained in this book.

Chapter 1 laid out the argument as to why expansive education is needed today.

Chapter 2 defined the field of expansive education. It charted the history of the ideas behind it and listed some of the thinkers on whose shoulders expansive educators sit. It also explored the contribution from the learning sciences to our understanding of the emerging field of expansive education. This chapter also clearly distinguished between progressive and expansive education. In the case of the latter there is an unambiguous commitment to both the cultivation of 21st century dispositions for learning and living *and* also to improved attainment in examinations and tests.

Chapter 3 offered a proof of concept as shown by examples drawn from different countries and, in a few cases, from national education ministries. It also described ways in which teachers are increasingly seeing their role as researchers, including those who have already become part of the Expansive Education Network.

Chapter 4 explored the concept of expansive pedagogy, seeking to spell out the ten kinds of choices that teachers can take which can make it more likely that expansive learning will take place in their classrooms.

Actions

Finally, in this chapter, from our analysis of the theories and practices of implementing expansive education in the real world, we identify a set of actions which we believe follow from our assumptions and analysis. Many of these are precisely the kinds of things we have described throughout this book, especially the actions of our pioneers whose stories appear in Chapter 3.

At the end of the present chapter, on page 191, we bring all of these actions together and shape them into our call to action.

But before we articulate these actions, we have two more things to do. We need to understand some of the actual barriers experienced by our pioneers in the field; and we need to take a step back, in the light of one of these identified barriers—teachers themselves—to consider how best we can help teachers change to become more expansive.

Barriers to change in schools

Expansive education organisations, educational institutions and teachers have much to contend with in bringing expansive philosophies to learners. The most dominant factor relates to the status quo of education systems the world over. QED's Director of Learning Platforms articulates this really clearly:

> *Education systems have long histories of sustained practices through the process of enculturation from one generation to the one after. For example, the pervasiveness of the textbook / lecture model for learning is passed on from one generation of teachers to the next through the passive process of students sitting in such classes. Even innovative teachers may struggle to implement another way of doing things, or feel powerless to bring about effective change within the organization they work. As a result, the effort of transforming educational practices is akin to turning a battleship on a dime. It just doesn't work that way.*

Adding fuel to the fire are the current policies and nationally driven requirements for accountability and the raising of 'achievement' in 'core' academic subjects in many countries across the world. Even though expansive educators see their practices leading to both better learning and improved attainment, it can be hard for them to carry those who are solely performance-driven. Nevertheless, an increasing number of expansive educators are recognising that 'game one'— raising attainment in examinations—can best be achieved by focusing on 'game two'—realising the true objectives of an education in the 21st century, which centre around those learning dispositions that will stand children and young people in good stead in the real world.

Organisations promoting expansive education have identified various barriers to implementing expansive practices, some of which are external (restrictive policy, assessment and accountability systems which value other things and lack of funding, for example) and some internal (lack of understanding, lack of time, lack of leadership, restrictive teacher mindsets, inflexible curriculum organisation, etc.). Of course, the kinds of issues we are discussing here relate to almost all aspects of changing practice in education today. In looking at barriers, we are deliberately seeing them through the lens of a school, although many of the organisations we have been working with are beyond school and see at least part of their role as advocating change more broadly and so making it easier for schools to adopt expansive practices.

External barrier: perceptions of 'what counts'

A major external barrier is the perception that expansive education does not somehow fit with government policy, with what counts in the eyes of external accountability bodies, with assessment systems especially where examination results are converted into league tables of performance and so forth. Even if an expansive education organisation provides a service that impacts positively on children and young people's learning dispositions and academic success, official organisations are, more often than not, unable to endorse them. The Leonardo Effect has received praise from inspectorates and curriculum bodies, but these are unable officially to back independent initiatives. This means expansive organisations may need to grow from the 'bottom up' through word-of-mouth and marketing activities rather than through 'top down' support.

From a school's perspective, barriers to bringing in expansive practices sometimes reflect perception more than they do reality. Philosophy4Children, for example, commented that in the United Kingdom there is often a perceived need to stick rigidly to the National Curriculum to the point where teachers experience anxiety about their children attaining certain National Curriculum levels. Such teachers are unable to see how philosophy can be fitted into the rigid structure of the Curriculum and, therefore, do not attempt to do so. Here, it is the perception as much as the reality of external disapproval.

Schools, naturally, tend to focus on what is assessed externally. Where the goals of expansive education organisations are not seen as linking clearly to external targets, and their achievements are not counted in official statistics, schools under pressure can be tempted to focus on those things that are more obviously rewarded. This is not always the case, and forward-thinking school leaders will prioritise initiatives they believe are of value. For example, Learning Through Landscapes notices that teachers want to be able to teach outside as well as in, and are increasingly open to considering what might happen if they *don't* take a risk with learning. Similarly, SAPERE finds that 'more and more schools are prioritising P4C as they recognise the value of the impact that can be achieved'.

Nevertheless, not all schools recognise—or believe they can afford to recognise—the importance of expansive approaches. This can be particularly concerning for organisations, such as ASDAN in the United Kingdom, whose qualifications have been removed from the list that makes up school performance tables from 2014 onwards, and who suggests there is likely to be a major impact upon whether schools regard their Certificate of Personal Effectiveness qualification to be viable for large numbers of their pupils.

The Centre for Science Education in England is impacted similarly by the reduced level of focus that science receives as a subject at primary level since the removal of high-stakes testing at the end of primary education. It has seen a reduction in the amount of time dedicated to developing science in schools. As a consequence, the focus on developing personal capabilities for science learning (also no longer embraced by the National Curriculum) has further diminished.

Wherever high-stakes testing of academic subjects is emphasised— especially at the expense of a focus on learning dispositions or a broader range of subjects—the perceived urgency for adopting expansive approaches is diminished for all but the most future-focused teachers and school leaders. Future-focused leaders include those at Los Angeles' DaVinci Academy, who recognise that while state and national assessments may accurately capture specific skills and knowledge, there are other skill sets, vital to learning and real-world success, that cannot be measured in this way.

It is recognised universally in expansive circles that expansive education is not a 'nice to have' but is, in fact, the best approach to help children and young people learn and, as a by-product, to produce high test scores. Despite this knowledge, schools—even those who pride themselves in delivering an expansive education—find that exam pressure is a distinct barrier. In the world of high-stakes testing, DaVinci Academy finds that assessments themselves can create a degree of 'anxiety and other emotional hindrances for learning within students and teachers alike' and thus 'impede upon the ability of an educator to create meaningful learning experiences'. The Professional Development Secretary at England's prestigious Eton College agrees: 'Assessment is also focused more on subject skills and content than "expansive" dispositions and the pressure of exams limits teacher confidence on shifting to an expansive approach'. The RSA Academy, while keen to promote the view that head teachers do not need to choose between high levels of achievement (as traditionally measured) and a competence-based curriculum, realises that 'this is a difficult argument to win, both with some schools and also with government'.

For expansive education organisations that are not direct providers of child education, the theme is common and outside of their control. A number of organisations comment about this. First, Learning through Landscapes:

> *The pressure on schools to achieve high numbers of pupils attaining well in the academic exams will reduce the time and space given to children to build on their social and interactive skills, both areas which lend themselves well to being promoted through outside activity.*

Then, Mastering Learning:

Many of the teachers and administrators I speak with indicate how they and their schools are evaluated based on how students perform on national and state standardized assessments. While they think teaching students how to learn is important, the priority is on preparing students for successful performance on these standardized tests.

I am currently reaching out to local high schools, school districts and universities to educate them on the importance of enabling students to better understand the learning process and how, with this knowledge, students can be successful in any learning situation. Much of the reaction that I receive is that the priority is enabling the student to perform well on standardized tests, as mentioned above.

And Mindset Works:

In the current educational climate, schools feel tremendous pressure to produce outcomes on achievement tests. The idea of expansive education, though widely appealing, often takes a back seat. That is, while schools, districts and teachers may value this approach, it can be difficult for them to introduce it in their schools, given the demand for short-term increases in scores.

And finally, TASC:

Add to that the current wave of reforms that overinflate the value of necessary but inadequate test scores as the means for charting and measuring growth, and the challenge of reframing the conversations about teaching and learning can be all the more daunting. Not to mention changing practices on a system-wide level. The more that corporate interests set the terms of reforms

and developments in the education sector, the more difficult it
becomes to talk about, much less enact, transformative practices
that are as defined by qualitative results as they are by quantitative
data.

[There is a] lack of tested, accepted assessment tools that
measure essential skills and learning habits beyond standardized
tests of math and English.

Learning through Landscapes notices how concerning trends in education will affect the future workforce. The same trends and pressures could also affect how successful the organisation is in recruiting schools. It argues that current politics in the United Kingdom are pushing children towards a more rote-based learning system that is well suited to desks in rows in an indoor classroom. Exams are returning to the academic-based clinical subjects with single exam outcomes rather than the more accessible portfolio-based learning, which, it argues, 'will remove some of the options for the development of land-based skills best taught in the outdoors'. This trend is likely to 'have a significant impact on our future workforce as the number of young adults entering the agricultural workplace is dropping at a time when we need more recruits'.

Narrow views about the purpose of education and the importance assigned to achievement in high status 'academic' subjects is not confined to some policy makers and educators. Learning Futures makes the point that society at large has a role to play too:

We have to expand the minds of parents and students to see that
an overly narrow focus on examination results and Ofsted
approval is not serving the long-term prospects of our young
people. Increasing numbers of young people are struggling to
adapt to the habits of mind needed for higher education and the
world of work.

Misunderstanding about what expansive education seeks to be and to do can mean that it is seen as a luxury by many, rather than being at the core of good learning, whatever the subject content. To remedy this, expansive education organisations must 'convey that the expansive education approach is at the *heart* of learning—it's what motivates students to learn and guides and sustains their learning' (Mindset Works) and must 'come together to present coherent argument for an education system which seeks to prepare young people with the knowledge and skills which will be needed in an entrepreneurial future' (Learning Futures).

The outlook is not totally bleak, however. The Curriculum Foundation believes that while some schools are concerned about examination results and the opinion of official school inspectors to the detriment of all else,

> *most recognise that they are not in a 'either–or' situation, and that the best route to exam success and Ofsted approval is high quality learning within a dynamic curriculum that engages pupils' interest and excites their imaginations.*

External barrier: lack of funding

Cost pressures sometimes restrict what expansive education organisations are able to do. Pressures in the economy that lead to inevitable cuts in spending on education within the public sector can mean that schools are less willing to take perceived risks. Or they may consider themselves less able to invest in the necessary resources or teaching cover needed to enable teachers to invest time in training. The first to be squeezed are those activities perceived as non-core, including outdoor activities. In London, outdoor experience provider Widehorizons says that adventure is seen as being something beyond the school gate and is not provided for by the state, so this can prevent schools from adopting its services.

In the United States, TASC finds that a lack of dedicated public funding streams to aid their particular area of investment means that if schools want assistance they need to draw on multiple education and youth development funds, each of which has its own regulations and limitations.

CFEE delivers free conferences for educators and parents from both public and private schools in the United States, bringing in inspirational speakers from around the world. Funding for such events is dependent upon support from schools and is, by its nature, limited.

In Scotland, the Association of Chartered Teachers finds that some councils are reluctant to spend money to pay for the extra salary associated with employing a Chartered Teacher.

In an increasingly networked world, schools without sufficient access to information about expansive education practices are at a disadvantage. CUREE, whose raison d'être is to promote the use of research in practice, finds that many schools do not know what other schools are doing, what is available on the market, what works or where to find information on these issues.

Where new ideas are involved, change can be slow. The University of Aberdeen's Participation in Learning course leader cites reasons such as internal school politics, a culture clash (be it at personal, professional, school or local authority level), a lack of leadership within schools, peer resistance to change, lack of pupil skills and motivation, structural barriers such as timetabling and organisational factors including assessment, workloads and competing priorities. TASC adds to this the preconceptions held by staff about the degree to which change is possible: to what degree might we change scheduling, staffing or curriculum, for example? Schools often tend to keep new ideas on the fringes of the regular timetable. Learning Futures cites 'challenge weeks' or 'project Fridays' as examples.

Timetabling and the siloing of subjects contribute to structural barriers in schools. The Centre for Science Education finds that secondary schools often struggle to take a cross-departmental approach to the development of the skills required for learning. Curriculum timetabling gets in the way to the point where schools are unclear how to squeeze philosophical approaches to learning into the school day (SAPERE) or how to combine subjects into a cross-curricular approach (The Leonardo Effect).

We have already mentioned perceived risks. Nervousness on the part of teachers, or, more often perhaps, ingrained in school culture, may be exacerbated by financial or political factors such as a lack of funds (risky activities get sidelined) or by a focus on exams (again, risky activities are put on hold). Nevertheless, perception of risk and the idea that 'teachers can be nervous about taking pupils outdoors for fear they will "disappear"' (Learning Through Landscapes) is something that can probably be tackled successfully at school level.

Internal barriers: teachers, their mindsets and their learning needs

The biggest single barrier we found to progress within schools is teachers themselves. All of the external pressures we have listed in the last few pages can find expression in the teacher's mind. Many teachers are naturally conservative and, once habituated into ways of doing things, can be extremely reluctant to shift their practices.

Of course this is not helped by initial teacher education, which almost completely ignores expansive education in most countries. The RSA Academy finds that initial teacher training (as the education required prior to service in the classroom is referred to in the United Kingdom) does not develop the teaching styles or approaches to teaching and learning that are required of the RSA's own teachers. For example: 'The willingness, on occasion, to teach out of their own subject area; the understanding of the competences and how they can be effective in improving learning'.

The Leonardo Effect comments perceptively that initial teacher training often mirrors the school experience and, as such, produces new teachers, many of whom consider examination success to be the only criteria for successful schools. Notions of learning dispositions, growth mindset, expandable intelligence, metacognition and the like are frequently ones that new teachers are only introduced to by chance when they happen to meet colleagues for whom these are central beliefs. This situation has to be addressed at the source: many universities and teaching colleges will need to shift their thinking. 'It is essential that opinion-formers in education realise and propagate the understanding that creative teaching and learning allows skills and knowledge to be imparted simultaneously'.

Trends in the education of society can lead to a depletion of vital skills. For the Philosophy Foundation, its greatest barrier to success is a shortage of philosophy graduates. With a small pool of graduates, a long lead-time for training and a lack of guaranteed work for them, the Foundation has a struggle to recruit from both supply and demand perspectives.

Teachers themselves can stand in the way of schools developing expansive approaches, particularly if good leadership is lacking. Key factors are teachers' fears, their level of understanding, their willingness to invest time and effort and their access to research.

Some teachers lack confidence when it comes to trying out new approaches. They may find a great deal of security in their assumed role as 'sage on the stage', seemingly protected by the understanding that they are the holder of knowledge, and comfortable in their assumed role as imparter of that knowledge. When tasked with taking a constructivist stance to learning and standing back into the role of facilitator, many teachers may be moved too far beyond their comfort zone to relish the challenge.

Other teachers lack understanding of the rationale behind expansive approaches. According to ASDAN: 'Some teachers need a lot of support and development work to really get the essence of "guided reflection" and the coaching conversation!' While Learning through Landscapes suggests that: 'Many have not had the skills taught at teacher training level to enable them to think about utilising outdoor spaces in their day-to-day activity'.

Still others are unwilling to change the status quo and want to remain doing what they always have, opting 'to continue in the same vein and teach in the same ways that have always "worked"' (Eton College). For some, this is because some expansive approaches can require much commitment and hard work. Training can be challenging and can reflect only the start of a journey, the demands of which 'are often beyond the reach of some teachers' (SAPERE).

Regardless of their stance towards expansive education, lack of access to current, digestible research can be a barrier to teachers. CUREE's 2011 survey[3] of over 1000 practitioners found that access to research was a significant obstacle for teachers trying to focus on their own continuing professional development. Lack of support from school leadership was cited as further obstruction that prevented teachers from engaging in, and engaging with, research.

Stories of success

By contrast, we found many common themes among the success stories from our pioneering colleagues. The greatest successes are often seen where whole-school training is given over to a particular approach. SAPERE finds schools can support the approach better by implementing a positive school policy statement, and notes particular successes where schools are linked together through networks so that there is a degree of continuity as children progress through the education system. Indeed, Eton College finds it essential that feeder schools embrace an expansive approach. The Leonardo Effect finds that they are often contacted for help by schools or local authorities who have heard head teachers speaking about their approach at local 'cluster group' meetings between networked schools. Networking worldwide can also be of benefit. Learning Futures has established links with world-leading High Tech High Schools in San Diego.

Although expansive education is for all types of learners, Mindset Works reminds us that it is not just for struggling students:

> *Many of our 'brightest' students are afraid of challenges and do not know how to cope with difficulty and because of this may not fulfil their potential. It is also coming to light that many of the students at the top of our achievement distribution would not stack up well against the top students in other countries.*

Indeed, for the Centre for Science Education (CSE), building in systems for recognition and reward of personal skills and capabilities as part of the learning process is best achieved in schools where basic literacy and numeracy achievement is already good.

Government support can be instrumental in providing a boost to the vital work of expansive education organisations. Some governments recognise the importance of building expansive approaches into education of children and young people, and cooperate with expansive organisations, as we saw, for example, on page 82.

The Curriculum Foundation's approach, which focuses on building wider competencies into curricula, strikes a chord with most international governments, who are keen to see this happen in their own jurisdictions. International comparisons of education systems through PISA[††] rankings cause much concern to governments, and some governments are recognising the importance of building in this

---

[††] PISA—the Programme for International Student Assessment—is an international study, launched by the worldwide Organisation for Economic Co-operation and Development (OECD) in 1997. It assesses 15-year-olds' competencies in key subjects (reading, mathematics and science) every three years. To date, over 70 countries and economies have participated in the study. PISA provides global rankings as a way of attempting to show which educational systems are offering students the best training for entering the workforce in the future.

specific expansive approach to curriculum. The Foundation identifies the Shanghai region of China as well as South Korea as being highly successful jurisdictions that are both working with it to build competencies into the curriculum. Morocco is another case in point— its lower ranking sits alongside its own recognition that an expansive approach is the one most likely to improve overall learning. Scottish educational policy (the Curriculum for Excellence) also contributes to the continuation of the University of Aberdeen's exploration of participatory approaches, because schools and local authorities are able to appreciate that such approaches link directly to the Scottish curriculum.

Government support is valuable, as is support from specific inspectors and other members of educational governance but, for The Leonardo Effect, the most significant method by which schools have approached it for help has been word-of-mouth from head teachers and teachers who are pleased with its outcomes. Indeed, the support of head teachers is vital, and several organisations made this point to us. Philosophy4Children finds that commitment from head teachers is the key to getting philosophy-based approaches embedded into schools. Beyond support, Learning Futures finds that active participation of head teachers is critical. QED Foundation finds that schools will adopt tools and approaches they believe will help them to reach their own goals, suggesting that adoption is often due to visionary leadership, which may be on the part of administrators or teachers.

CSE suggests that if personal skills and capabilities are to be recognised and rewarded as part of the learning process, it is helpful if schools already use and recognise the value of active teaching and learning methods. Further, it helps if schools are already seeking to take more 'creative' or more 'child-led' approaches to curriculum rather than adopting 'bolt-on' approaches to competencies. This is far from rare, however, and CSE suggests that many schools are committed to enhancing curriculum provision through creative curriculum design, and realise the importance employers attach to capabilities such as self-management, teamwork, communication and problem solving.

Learning through Landscapes finds that if outdoor activities are to be valued, it helps that many schools are becoming increasingly receptive to adopting a 'risk–benefit' rather than a 'risk assessment' approach to decisions regarding potentially risky activities. A risk–benefit approach encourages schools to take into consideration the impact of not exposing a child to a potentially risky activity that could carry enormous learning potential.

Mindset Works has learned that sometimes the expansive education approach is misunderstood as being something that is just for 'less able' students or 'low achievers', or thought of as though it were a separate syllabus of content outside of the core and necessary knowledge and that this is to be avoided. In the United Kingdom, a similar view is held among some schools, who are concerned with examination results and the opinion of official inspectors.

CSE finds that if personal skills and capabilities are to be recognised and rewarded as part of the learning process, it is helpful if teachers are confident in their own pedagogy and feel supported by their colleagues. CUREE provides tools and resources to aid peer collaboration among teachers and finds that this method of providing support can overcome potential barriers to successful implementation of evidence-informed approaches to practice. Learning Futures suggests that it is important, however, that teachers (and senior leaders) are supported and challenged during the period where their professional practice is changing, if the innovations they put into place are to stick.

For expansive approaches to work, schools must recognise the need to be expansive in their culture, as well as in their approach to teaching and learning, by allowing teachers to try new approaches and test out what works in the classroom. Where teachers are given permission to experiment and be researchers, as well as teachers, Learning Futures finds that schools have noticed 'spectacular' improvements in engagement. While teacher autonomy can be positive, as pointed out by Eton College, autonomy also gives scope for teachers to teach in the same ways that have always seemed to work.

Philosophical approaches, like those offered by The Philosophy Foundation, Philsophy4Children and SAPERE, depend upon classroom teachers 'buying in' to the approach, and, says SAPERE, are more successful where teachers pursue their own understanding of Vygotskian ways of learning in order to help learners progress intellectually through learning dialogue. Where teachers take time to reflect upon the approach to teaching and enquiring, Philosophy4Children find they are more likely to adopt the approach. SAPERE's approach involves teachers working with colleagues to develop more philosophical teaching throughout the curriculum, so reflection on what works and how to push developments forward is very important.

There is, as we have seen throughout this book, a growing body of evidence to support the claims of expansive educators worldwide and wherever we have encountered such, we have cited it. Just one example of this is the University of the West of England's recently published report[4] investigating the impact of ASDAN's Certificate of Personal Effectiveness (CoPE) on GCSE attainment, to which we alluded on pages 88 and 89. The report found a statistically significant association with improved attainment in GCSE qualifications. The evidence suggests that CoPE mitigates the underachievement of individuals with serious educational challenges, and markedly improves the achievement of individuals without such challenges.

In 2010, CUREE published a report[5] commissioned by the Qualifications and Curriculum Development Agency to examine evidence from around the world relating to curriculum development. This large-scale international evidence base shows that curriculum experiences that effectively promote young people's learning and achievement:

▶   provide context-based learning experiences and link learning at school and in the home
▶   include structured group work and planning for effective talk
▶   foster a less compartmentalised approach to the curriculum to promote conceptual development and cross-curricular learning
▶   include planning for appropriate tasks that challenge every young person.

CUREE's evidence collated for the General Teaching Council pupil participation anthology[6] highlights the difference that student-focused environments make to young people's participation. These environments include effective questioning and feedback, group work, thinking skills, enquiry-based approaches and assessment for learning.

The Leonardo Effect takes a research-based approach to integrating science and art learning. It has run several evaluated pilot studies funded by, among others, NESTA and the Paul Hamlyn Foundation and claims that it has a 'proven interdisciplinary teaching methodology [that] delivers sustainable improvements in school and pupil performance'. Anecdotal evidence[7] from testimonials of head teachers, teachers, parents and pupils suggests that the approach can improve expansive outcomes: thinking skills, problem solving, creativity and independence, as well as a broader range of desirable outcomes including attainment, reading levels, motivation, confidence, engagement, factual learning and knowledge retention.

The RSA Academy's curriculum was developed as a result of the RSA's research and subsequent trial of a new approach to learning and to curriculum development. The RSA conducted some research in the mid 1990s about the future of work and the impact that those changes would have on the individual. One of the outcomes of that research was a first list of competences—capabilities that individuals would need to help them prosper in the 21st century. The next stage was a three-year trial in a small number of schools to ascertain whether the competences could contribute effectively to a school curriculum—the first indications of what a competence-based curriculum might look like and early impact of this new curriculum and style of learning on learners. This trial identified the potential benefits in terms of learning and engagement that would result from a competence-based education. As a result of positive outcomes of the trial[8] the competence-based curriculum was taken up by a larger number of schools, including the RSA's own RSA Academy.

CUREE tells us that evidence suggests that teachers are better enabled to take expansive approaches with young people if their own experience of professional development is expansive. A large-scale systematic review[9] aimed to fill the gap in evidence about linkages between teacher inquiry and learner outcomes. It highlighted that when teachers undertake inquiry and research, young people experience improved outcomes. These included knowledge and skill outcomes, behaviour outcomes and attitude, belief and motivation outcomes. Extensive evidence across the studies showed a link between teacher engagement with or in research, and these outcomes for learners.

Teacher research practices include:

▶ directly accessing research intelligence, for example, through websites, reading groups, researcher-in-school schemes, as well as in journals and other print media
▶ participating in externally generated research studies
▶ undertaking research as part of their accredited professional studies
▶ undertaking specific teacher researcher activities outside accredited study
▶ actively experimenting in their own classrooms using a reflective–evaluative enquiry approach

▶ working in pairs or groups to read, analyse and discuss research relevant to professional and school development, and to design collaborative studies within or even across schools.

The After-School Corporation's (TASC) ExpandED Schools program aims to improve schools and communities, close the achievement gap, raise graduation rates, combat the 'STEM‡‡ crisis' and build school–community partnerships. It claims that:

> *Dozens of empirical studies from the past decade show the same results, particularly among disadvantaged students: more learning time, in the form of high-quality after-school and summer programs, leads to greater achievement, better school attendance and more enthusiastic learners.*[10]

An independent four-year study[11] of TASC's after-school programs showed improved achievement in maths, improved attendance and improved attitudes towards learning. The most important practice to be linked to learner gains in both maths and reading/English language was 'high frequency and duration of activities focusing on academics and cognitive development'.[12] Demonstrating that an expansive education is key to academic success, such activities were achieved most successfully through expansive projects that used 'extended, multidisciplinary activities, often involving groups of students working together and also often culminating in performances or major products or publications'.[13]

In other words, success comes not from extending the school day, but from expansive use of time during that expanded period of time. A core element of the ExpandED Schools program is its recognition that

---

‡‡ STEM is an acronym for the fields of study within the four categories: science, technology, engineering and mathematics.

'four out of five elementary teachers say reading and math are crowding out other subjects'.[14] Extra time allows for a more balanced focus on STEM learning, hands-on collaboration and problem solving, physical education and exercise, arts education and interdisciplinary approaches.

We should never underestimate the power of intelligent school advocacy. Here is a Philosophy4Children school shouting its excitement and success from the rooftop:

> It revolutionised our school, and the skills that the children acquired during the philosophy sessions were used across the whole curriculum. Their ability to question and to articulate their thoughts gave them confidence and a passion for learning. Adults took them seriously and saw their less academic, as well as academic, pupils thrive. It changes the dynamic of an institution in which children's ability to learn is not dependent on a good memory but is built on ideas and thinking that are both deep and challenging. Once children are hooked into this new way of thinking, they become citizens who are excited about learning—with a thirst for knowledge that becomes a permanent part of their lives.

When all is said and done, expansive education is about a change of mindset with regard to what matters, what it means to be smart and where school learning can take place. And the minds that need to be changed, if it is to be implemented in schools, are the teachers'.

Changing teachers' habits

Changing any engrained pattern of behaviour is hard work. It requires a real understanding of what is to be changed, the ability to imagine the new way of behaving, the commitment to change and lots of practice in different situations to help the shift to become engrained enough. For some while, the 'new' way of doing something feels just that, new. And it is all too easy to slip back into old, familiar ways of doing things. Here we review a few of the more important considerations we sought to bear in mind, drawing on a piece of research we undertook during which we specifically explored teacher habit change.[15]

An important starting point is the appreciation that the more precisely the proposed habit change can be understood, the more likely it will happen. All too often, initiatives fail because the participants do not clearly understand exactly what they need to do, when they need to do it and how they can be supported through the process. Understanding needs to take place at both the theoretical level ('We are trying to create an expansive learning environment because the research suggests that this may help to create better learners') and, equally importantly, at the practical level ('Three practical tips for giving feedback: look for what's going well, try and ask questions and don't tell people what to do').

One way of increasing the likelihood of things learned subsequently being used is by imagining your actions before you try them for real. Peter Gollwitzer and others[16] have shown that anticipatory 'implementation intentions'—imagining what you might do in a certain situation—significantly increase the likelihood of intentions being translated into actions. In other words, the more you can imagine and anticipate a change in your behaviour, the better. In terms of teacher development, this might suggest role-play and simulation activities as well as more explicit visualisation of new experiences, all coupled with plenty of opportunities for recourse to the experiences and guidance of other colleagues.

Throughout this book, we have explored not just the practical aspects of classroom activity but also the culture within which such activities sit. This is very true in schools, where the creation of a culture in which teachers are empowered to experiment with active encouragement from senior leaders is an important part of the mix.

For, it turns out, just by becoming familiar with something, it is likely that we will become positively engaged. Known as the 'mere exposure effect' and discovered by Robert Zajonc[17], we know that creating an atmosphere in which new ways of doing things can safely be experienced is a key element of successful habit change.

And then there is the absolute necessity of mutual support and collegiality. Alcoholics Anonymous, Weight Watchers and many other similar groups gather together precisely because they know that one person trying to change is much less likely to succeed than a group of people embarking upon a similar endeavour. The same is true of teachers, where such groups are likely to be known by a variety of different terms of which 'professional learning community' is one of the most widely used. Research studies attest to the power of social support and social commitment in successful habit change.[18]

In an educational context, the importance of learning communities and learning cultures has been well researched by Louise Stoll and colleague[19] and by Dylan Wiliam.[20] We began to explore Wiliam's findings earlier on page 41, and we return to them here. It is much easier, he argues, to get teachers to change when we think precisely about the preferred actions we want to perform and then focus on them, just as we were trying to do in the last chapter, when we focused on the ten dimensions of expansive pedagogy.

It is also critically important to realise that the process of building understanding takes time and practise. Phillippa Lally and colleagues[21] have found that it takes around two months of concerted practice before a simple habit change (eating a piece of fruit after lunch, say) becomes stabilised. Needless to say, habit change in teaching style is more complex than regular fruit consumption, but the timescale issue is a really important one. Wiliam argues that it takes at least two years for a group of teachers trying to shift practice with respect to something complex.[22] (His example is formative assessment, which is not a bad proxy for aspects of expansive education.)

When teachers are invited to change their practices from more traditional (restrictive) methods to more expansive ones, they are being invited to rethink their views about:

- what school is for
- the power of mindset
- themselves as learners.

Coupled with this may well be anxieties about their confidence levels when the focus shifts away from acquiring knowledge towards cultivating the dispositions in the context of specific subject-based or project-based activities.

The unit of change for most teachers is the lesson and teachers need to be sure enough that on Monday morning with a real class they can do what is required of them. But to get to this unit requires changes in teacher thinking and acting, both quantitatively (for example, on how many of our ten dimensions of expansive pedagogy is a teacher acting) and qualitatively (what kinds of change and to what extent are these embedded in practice).

We end by stressing that, as enquiry is a core principle of expansive education, we believe that there will be more questioning than telling in any change process. At the simplest level, it is important to sell enquiry and action research to teachers, for many of them are put off if they perceive it be too academic. John Macbeath and Graham Handscomb summarise the benefits by asking and answering the questions directly:

Why engage in research? Teachers researching their own schools and classroom have found it:
1. *encourages practitioners to question, explore and develop their practice*

2. *to be a highly satisfying and energising professional activity*
3. *has become an integral part of continuing professional development*
4. *has brought new insights, new levels of understanding and new challenges*
5. *has enhanced the quality of learning and teaching.*[23]

Such a list will not persuade a jaded or hostile teacher, but it may open up dialogue with a significant majority. We have found that more sceptical teachers often respond to more direct anticipation of the problems they are likely to encounter along the way.[24]

Some frequently aired doubts

Here are some common concerns and in each case we have suggested a *possible* line of response.

It sounds good but we can't risk damaging our examination results

The evidence shows the reverse. When learners are helped to become more confident, independent and articulate about the process of learning, the results go up, not down. Students can get good results through becoming more resilient and resourceful, as opposed to being more spoon-fed.

It's complicated and we can't afford the time

Anything worth doing takes time and expansive education is not a fad or a quick fix. Expansive education does not require teachers to rip up the rule book and start from scratch. It's a case of being sure that you spend your time helping young people both to do well in examinations and to become better learners.

Ofsted (or whichever the national school accountability body is) won't like it

This is an understandable but ungrounded fear. In fact the reverse is true. Ofsted in England (and others across the world) are increasingly interested in the quality of teaching and learning. An investment in expansive pedagogy is likely to make inspectors more, not less, impressed.

When we are observed or inspected we'll just revert to type even if we are trying to be more expansive for the rest of the time

If that happens, it's not the end of the world! Although, interestingly, schools have told us that playing it safe can sometimes mean that the lesson is less good than it would be if teachers were taking some reasonable risks.

Isn't expansive education just a fancy way of saying 'good teaching'? It's what we've always done

This depends on your definition of good teaching! Expansive education brings a degree of rigour to what works best in different contexts. Schools that truly embrace one of the approaches we have described in this book report that, in most cases, while they may have been doing some of what is suggested, they realise they had not been systematic or deep enough in what they were doing beforehand.

Expansive education sounds like the progressive education of the 1970s and 80s. It didn't work then and it won't work now

Much progressive education counters 'traditional' education by making a feature of its child-centredness, often giving learners far more control over what they learn and how they learn it. While expansive educators believe that learners need to be in the driving seat, they very much want learners to have a co-pilot coaching and guiding them—someone who oversees the whole journey and has a clear map for their journeys. Too often, progressive education was a reaction against the status quo and threw out the rigour, structure and guidance that all learners need. Learners will become more independent and self-organising through expansive education, but not in a thoughtless or haphazard way.

It's my job to give students the right answers, surely?

Yes, it is! They will need to get the 'right' answers to do well in many examinations. The critical issue here is *how* students get to the right answers. Helping learners to do things for themselves, not to be 'thrown' when they get asked a problem that is phrased slightly differently from what they have been practising—these are key life skills and good exam-passing techniques.

We've tried it and our students prefer to be spoon-fed

Some students undoubtedly do. But this may well be because it is all they have experienced in their education to date. Most learners prefer to be more actively involved, even if there is an initial resistance. If you start small, you will be able to build students' willing engagement.

We've done learning to learn and thinking skills. We don't need another initiative, thanks

The trouble with stand-alone courses is that they do not have much impact beyond the particular setting in which they happen. They tend to end up just tied to one specific content or context and not get used elsewhere.

Expansive education might be OK for the able students, but what about the less able?

This is a justifiable concern. Some of the concepts in expansive education may take some grasping. But at the heart of what we are saying when we draw on Carol Dweck's work is that self-belief matters. We can all develop growth mindsets, whatever our currently described level of 'ability'.

Expansive education might be OK for the less able students, but what about the more able?

Many 'high-fliers' are precisely the kinds of learners who, if they have 'fixed mindsets', do not fulfil their potential. Expanding the mindsets, opportunities and locations for gifted learners will stretch them even further and they will soar.

By the time students come to us, it's too late to shift their attitudes

It's never too late to learn new 'tricks', although the longer you have been doing something in one way, the more engrained it is as a habit of mind. Older students and older people can also benefit from being more involved with the processes of their learning.

Our parents wouldn't like it. They are very traditional

While some of the language may be unfamiliar, provided you take time to explain what you are doing to parents and make clear the ways in which it will help their children do better in tests and better in the real world, they become strong supporters.

Our kids come from such deprived backgrounds, it just wouldn't work

This is a counsel of despair that needs to be challenged head-on. It is as inappropriate to say this about expansive education as it is to make such an unproven link to any opportunity that you might choose to offer your students.

It's all very well but it's the child's ability that is the only thing that really makes a difference

If this were true, parents and teachers would be no more than 'filing clerks' in the great game of life. Luckily, it is not the case. This idea can be difficult to shift but shifting it is a challenge to which we simply have to rise as expansive educators.

***

We end our book with a call to action.

The call to action

The organisations featured in this book (and listed on page xiv) believe that expansive education is critically important for all children and all schools today, wherever they are in the world. As we learn more about what it is, what it might be, how it is being implemented and how it might be implemented even better, we are finding out much. Here are some of our 'essential learnings' for you to explore and use. They are by no means set in stone and we have created a forum where you can take part in helping us to shape them on www.expansiveeducation.net.

1. Understand the essence

Expansive education, as we are describing it, brings together a number of complementary approaches. But we are increasingly clear that its four components seem to bring added impact:

1. Developing expansive dispositions requires us to focus on what the broader purposes of school are and to be explicit about those dispositions that we believe will help students to get on at school *and* in the real world.

2. Demonstrating the learnability of intelligence seems to us to be a moral imperative if we are to help all learners be the best that they can become.

3. Going beyond school requires us to engage with parents, with the outdoors and with the host of organisations who can help teachers and learners to develop the dispositions and mindsets which will stand them in great stead for their lives.

4. Developing a community of enquiring teachers who see themselves as learners is essential if whole schools are going to adopt and embed expansive education.

Ivor Hickey, The Leonardo Effect Director, argues:

We see a serious need for expansive education in schools. Governments ask for transferrable skills to be developed to aid the production of lifelong learners, but assess only narrowly and with a focus on literacy. Learners who are weaker in this area often become disaffected and gain few qualifications. Learners who have strengths in literacy often do well in national examinations, but by concentrating on accumulation of factual knowledge to sit examinations miss out on the creative skills necessary both for employment and to succeed in higher education where there is less tendency to 'teach to the examination'. The great danger is that teacher education, which often mirrors school experience, will develop new teachers who genuinely think that examination success is the only criteria for successful schools. It is essential that opinion-formers in education realise and propagate the understanding that creative teaching and learning allows skills and knowledge to be imparted simultaneously.

In understanding the field, there are many branches of the learning sciences that colleagues may want to explore more and the references at the end of this book and the websites of our many pioneering colleagues may be a good place to start!

2. Make it the core of what you do

If you try and do anything half-heartedly in schools, it seldom works. When Carol McGuiness was reviewing some of the early work on thinking skills, she identified the three different ways in which such work can be introduced into schools: as a stand-alone program; embedding it in an individual subject; or infusing it across the whole life of the school. The last of these was then and remains still the more substantive way of approaching change of this kind. McGuiness counselled: 'Whatever approach is adopted, the methodology must ensure that the learning transfers beyond the context in which it occurs and embed it'.[25]

That an initiative needs to be fully adopted and not peripheral to a school's work is a lesson that many educators will recognise as both simple and profoundly important. Carol Dweck, in her role as co-founder of Mindset Works, put it to us more forcefully still:

> The expansive education approach is often misunderstood as a desire to teach students things that are not part of core learning. It is often seen as a luxury when human and financial resources are in short supply. It is important to convey that the expansive education approach is at the heart of learning—it's what motivates students to learn and guides and sustains their learning.

Once you really understand each of the four aspects of expansive education, it is difficult to imagine doing it half-heartedly. It needs to become the driving mission of a school's work.

3. Customise it

In this book, we have listed many different approaches to expansive education and sought to find connections between them. If we are to avoid confusing schools, it seems obvious to us that we must seek to make connections rather than advocating one specific approach over another (unless there is sound evidence for such a distinction).

Schools tell us that what they want is to be able to customise what we are all offering them and, provided their approach is itself coherent (has all or most of the four key elements of expansive education as we have defined it), we suggest that this makes good sense.

4. Play both games

Early on in the book we introduced the metaphor of the two games of school. Game one is about helping students get the best possible examination or test scores in whatever assessment jurisdiction they find themselves in. Game two is about identifying dispositions for thriving in life and actively seeking to cultivate these.

If expansive approaches are to find favour and take off we are convinced that we have to promote both of these games. Indeed, we have to draw on the evidence that shows how being better at game two leads to better results in game one (but not necessarily vice versa).

Brian Male, Director of The Curriculum Foundation, reminds us:

Schools and nations do not have to choose between high standards within subjects, and an education that prepares young people for life. It is possible to have both. An expansive curriculum can excite imaginations, widen horizons, raise aspirations, inspire creativity, deepen subject understanding and can lay the roots of lifelong learning. It can send all young people out into the world with the confidence, the ability and the desire to make that world a better place.

5. Build a wide platform of support

This book has been written to make a contribution to such a building project. The Expansive Education Network—www.expansiveeducation.net—

is the place we imagine this construction work being continued in over many years.

We need support from governments, states, local authorities, districts, schools, colleges, universities, parents, employers, research organisations and, of course, the many pioneering organisations out there who advocate aspects of expansive education.

Part of this coalition-building is also our own willingness to model the inquiry processes we are seeking to encourage, by constantly and non-defensively trying to marshal evidence of what is working and what is not working well enough and, above all, how expansive approaches can indeed develop the kinds of powerful learners we want to see emerging from our schools.

6. Involve students

One of our rules of thumb is to consistently overestimate (slightly) the extent to which students can take responsibility for, and think about, their own learning. If we do, the vast majority will delight us with their ability to manage, organise and evaluate learning for themselves, and astound us with the quality and maturity of their thinking. They can also be our most effective allies, whether demonstrating their ability to coach others or explaining what expansive education is to parents.

7. Focus on teachers

We also advocate acknowledging explicitly the changed roles for teachers. The previous chapter showed some of the ways in which teachers can choose to do things differently in their classrooms. But knowledge or even skill is not enough. Just as with young people, teachers have to have the disposition to teach differently. Part of our work with teachers requires us to recognise that habit change is hard and to use some of the techniques we have discussed earlier.

***

We leave almost the last word to one of our pioneers, David Price from Learning Futures: 'I hope your book will expand minds to challenge the dreary, regressive direction in which we're currently headed'.

Education has to change. It has to engage the energies and intelligence of all young people. It has to respond to their anxieties about the future, and to help them develop the mental, emotional and social equipment they will need to thrive in a complex, challenging and exciting world. Here's hoping, as David Price says, that the seeds of expansive education that we have explored in this book will continue to germinate strongly and to populate the earth!

References

Foreword

1   G Lakoff, *Know your values and frame the debate*, Chelsea Green Publishing, White River Junction, Vermont, 2004, p. xv.
2   V Boix Mansilla & A Jackson, *Educating for global competence: preparing our youth to engage the world*, Council of Chief State School Officers' EdSteps Initiative & Asia Society Partnership for Global Learning, New York, 2011.
3   L Vygotsky, *Mind in society: the development of higher psychological processes*, Harvard University Press, Cambridge, Massachusetts, 1978.
4   http//www.todayinsci.com/M/Medawar_Peter/MedawarPeter-Quotations.htm

Chapter 1

1   D Perkins, *Outsmarting IQ: the emerging science of learnable intelligence*, The Free Press, New York, 1995.
2   R Baumeister & J Tierney, *Will power: rediscovering our greatest strength*, Allan Lane, London, 2012.
3   B Lucas & G Claxton, *New kinds of smart: how the science of learnable intelligence is changing education*, Open University Press, Berkshire, 2010.
4   L Resnick, 'Learning in school and out', *Educational Researcher*, vol. 16, no. 9, 1987, pp. 13–20.
5   A Sullivan, 'Notes from a marine biologist's daughter: on the art and science of attention', *Harvard Educational Review*, vol. 70, no. 2, 2000, pp. 211–27.
6   J Hattie, *Visible learning: a synthesis of over 800 meta-analyses relating to achievement*, Routledge, London, 2009, p. 22.
7   www.expansiveeducation.net
8   http://www.thinkingschool.co.uk/

9   We first discussed this concept in C Claxton, B Lucas & R Webster, *Bodies of knowledge*, Edge Foundation, London, 2010. We develop it in more detail on pp. 17–20 of that book.

10   '"Spoonfed" students lack confidence at Oxbridge', *Times Educational Supplement*, 10 December 2010, http://www.tes.co.uk/article.aspx?storycode=6065624.

11   ibid.

12   D Perkins, 'Post-primary education has little impact on informal reasoning', *Journal of Educational Psychology*, vol. 77, no. 5, 1985, pp. 562–71.

13   http://www.instituteforhabitsofmind.com/

14   http://www.buildinglearningpower.co.uk/

15   A 5th Grader's graduation address, cited in AC Costa & B Kallick, *Discovering and exploring habits of mind*, ASCD, Alexandria, Virginia, 2000, p. xvi.

16   A Schleicher, *PISA 2006: science competences for tomorrow's world*, OECD, Paris, 2007.

17   http://www.thinkingschool.co.uk/

18   http://www.old-pz.gse.harvard.edu/vt/VisibleThinking_html_files/VisibleThinking1.html

19   http://www.wholeeducation.org/pages/story/who_is_involved/55,406/flow_foundation_.html

20   http://www.philosophy4children.co.uk/

21   http://www.ibo.org/

22   E de Corte, 'Historical developments in the understanding of learning', in H Dumon, D Istance, & F Benavides (eds), *The nature of learning: using research to inspire practice*, OECD, Paris, 2010, p. 45.

23   W Mischel, EB Ebbeson & AR Zeiss, 'Cognitive and attentional mechanisms in delay of gratification', *Journal of Personality and Social Psychology*, vol. 21, no. 2, 1972, pp. 204–18.

24   K Vohs & R Baumeister (eds), *Handbook of self-regulation: research, theory, and applications*, 2nd edn, Guilford, New York, 2011.

25   For a comprehensive overview of these, see B Lucas & G Claxton, *Wider skills for learning: what are they, how can they be cultivated, how could they be measured and why are they important for innovation?*, NESTA, London, 2009.

26   http://www.ibo.org/programmes/documents/learner_profile_en.pdf

Chapter 2

1 L Resnick, 'Making America smarter', *Education Week Century Series*, v. 18, no. 40, 1999, pp. 38–40.

2 Y Engeström, *Learning by expanding: an activity-theoretical approach to developmental research*, Orienta-Konsultit, Helsinki, 1987.

3 Y Engeström, 'Non scolae sed vitae discimus: toward overcoming the encapsulation of school learning', *Learning and Instruction*, vol. 1, 1991, pp. 243–59.

4 K Holzkamp, *Lernen: Subjektwissenschaftliche Grundlegung*, Campus Verlag, Frankfurt, 1993.

5 Pestalozzi, cited in M Dahwan, *Philosophy of Education*, Isha Books, Delhi, 2005, p. 186.

6 F Fröbel, *On the education of man*, Wienbrach, Keilhau/Leipzig, 1826, p. 2.

7 T Finser, 'Introduction', in R Steiner, *The roots of education: foundations of Waldorf education*, 3rd edn, Anthroposophic Press, New York, 1997, p. viii.

8 M Montessori, *The absorbent mind*, The Theosophical Publishing House, Madras, 1946, p. 206.

9 J Piaget, *The origins of intelligence in children*, WW Norton & Company, New York, 1936, p. 6.

10 J Bruner, *The culture of education*, Harvard University Press, Cambridge, Massachusetts, 1996, pp. viii–x.

11 R Feuerstein, *Feuerstein Institute*, Jerusalem, 2013, http://en.feuerstein-global.org/about-the-system.

12 J Dewey, 'My pedagogic creed', *School Journal*, vol. 54, 1987, pp. 77–80.

13 J Campbell, *Theorising habits of mind as a framework for learning*, paper presented at AARE 2006 International Education Research conference, Adelaide, 2007, p. 5.

14 C Rogers, *Client-centered therapy: its current practice, implications and theory*, Constable, London, 1957.

15 D Kolb, *The learning style inventory: technical manual*, McBer, Boston, Massachusetts, 1976.

16 D Schön, *The reflective practitioner: how professionals think in action*, Temple Smith, London, 1983.

17   D Schön, 'The theory of inquiry: Dewey's legacy to education', Curriculum Inquiry, vol. 22, no. 2, 1992, pp. 119–39.

18   L Resnick, 'Learning in school and out', Educational Researcher, vol. 16, no. 9, 1987, pp. 13–20.

19   L Resnick, 1999, op. cit.

20   See L Abramson, M Seligman & J Teasdale, 'Learned helplessness in humans: critique and reformulation', Journal of Abnormal Psychology, vol. 87, no. 1, 1978, p. 49, for an early description of this phenomenon.

21   H Gardner, Frames of mind: the theory of multiple intelligences, Basic Books, New York, 1993, p. xxxiii.

22   D Perkins & G Salomon, 'Rocky roads to transfer: rethinking mechanisms of a neglected phenomenon', Educational Psychologist, vol. 24, no. 2, 1989, pp. 113–42.

23   D Perkins, Outsmarting IQ: the emerging science of learnable intelligence, The Free Press, New York, 1995, p. 19.

24   D Perkins, Making learning whole: how seven principles of teaching can transform education, Jossey-Bass, San Francisco, 2009, p. 2.

25   R Sternberg, Successful intelligence: how practical and creative intelligence determine success in life, Simon & Schuster, New York, 1996, p. 127.

26   C Dweck, Mindset: the new psychology of success, Ballantine Books, New York, 2006.

27   ibid., p. 21.

28   ibid., p. 6.

29   G Colvin, Talent is overrated: what really separates world-class performers from everybody else, Nicholas Brealey, London, 2008.

30   D Coyle, The talent code: greatness isn't born, Arrow Books, London, 2010.

31   D Pink, Drive: the surprising truth about what motivates us, Riverhead Books, New York, 2009.

32   M Syed, Bounce: the myth of talent and the power of practice, Fourth Estate, London, 2010.

33   K Ericsson, R Krampe & C Tesch-Römer, 'The role of deliberate practice in the acquisition of expert performance', Psychological Review, vol. 100, no. 3, 1993, pp. 363–406.

34   M Gladwell, Outliers: the story of success, Little, Brown, Boston, 2008.

35 E Langer, *The power of mindful learning*, Addison-Wesley, Reading, Massachusetts, 1997.

36 E Langer, 'Mindfulness and Mindlessness', *Itineraries*, Second Journey, North Carolina, Summer, 2008, http://secondjourney.org/newsltr/ Archives/LangerE_08Sum.htm

37 K Robinson, *Ken Robinson says schools kill creativity*, online talk, TED, New York, 2006, http://www.ted.com/talks/ken_robinson_says_ schools_kill_creativity.html

38 E Wenger, *Communities of practice: a brief introduction*, June 2006, http://www.ewenger.com/theory/

39 M Fullan, 'Why teachers must become change agents', *Educational Leadership*, vol. 50, no. 6, 1993, pp. 12–17.

40 R Pascale, *Managing on the edge: how the smartest companies use conflict to stay ahead*, Simon & Schuster, New York, 1990, p. 14.

41 B Levin, *How to change 5000 schools: a practical and positive approach for leading change at every level*, Harvard Education Press, Cambridge, Massachusetts, 2008.

42 G Masters, *National school improvement tool*, Australian Council for Educational Research, Camberwell, 2012, p. 6.

43 D Wiliam, 'Changing classroom practice', *Informative Assessment*, vol. 65, no. 4, 2008, pp. 36–42.

44 ibid.

45 J Hattie, *Visible learning: a synthesis of over 800 meta-analyses relating to achievement*, Routledge, London, 2009.

46 J Hattie, *Visible learning for teachers: maximising impact on learning*, Routledge, London, 2012, pp. 14–15.

47 C De Simone, 'Problem-based learning: a framework for prospective teachers' pedagogical problem-solving', *Teacher Development*, vol. 12, no. 3, 2008, pp. 179–91.

48 See http://educationendowmentfoundation.org.uk/toolkit/

49 D Hargreaves, *Creating a self-improving school system*, National College for Leadership of Schools and Children's Services, Nottingham, 2010, p. 15.

50 C Watkins, E Carnell, C Lodge, P Wagner & C Whalley, 'Learning about learning enhances performance', *NSIN Research Matters*, National School Improvement Network, Institute of Education, University of London, no. 13, 2001.

51   M James, cited in C Watkins, 'Learning, performance and improvement', *INSI Research Matters*, International Network for School Improvement, Institute of Education, University of London, no. 34, 2010, p. 11.

52   G Claxton, *Learning to learn: the fourth generation*, TLO, Bristol, 2004.

53   ibid, p. 17.

54   JH Flavell, 'Metacognitive aspects of problem solving', in LB Resnick (ed.), *The nature of intelligence*, Erlbaum, Hillsdale, New Jersey, 1976, pp. 231–6.

55   M Csikszentmihalyi, *Flow and the psychology of discovery and invention*, Harper Perennial, San Francisco, 2013.

56   A Hargreaves, *Teaching in the knowledge society: education in the age of insecurity*, Open University Press, New York, 2003, p. 3.

57   A Biswas & C Gordon-Graham (eds.), *Rabindranath Tagore: a creative unity*, The Tagore Centre, London, 2006.

Chapter 3

1   R Ritchhart, *Intellectual character: what it is, why it matters and how to get it*, Jossey-Bass, San Francisco, California, 2001, p. xxii.

2   http://www.expansiveeducation.net

3   http://www.pz.harvard.edu/

4   http:/www.winchester.ac.uk/realworldlearning

5   See D Perkins, *Outsmarting IQ: the emerging science of learnable intelligence*, The Free Press, New York, 1995.

6   CBI, *First steps: a new approach for our schools. Ambition [noun] a desire and determination to achieve success*, Confederation of British Industry, London, 2012, p. 8.

7   http://www.expansiveeducation.net

8   R Ritchhart, M Church, & K Morrison, *Making thinking visible*, Jossey-Bass, San Francisco, 2011.

9   A Costa & B Kallick, *Discovering and exploring habits of mind*, ASCD, Alexandria, Virginia, 2002.

10   A Biemiller & D Meichenbaum, 'The nature and nurture of the self-directed learner', *Educational Leadership*, vol. 50, no. 2, 1992, pp. 75–80.

11   http://www.instituteforhabitsofmind.com/

12   Qualifications and Curriculum Development Agency, *A framework of personal learning and thinking skills*, Department for Children, Schools and Families, London, 2007.

13   http://www.curriculumfoundation.org/

14   Partnership for 21st Century Skills, 'Our mission', 2011, http://www.p21.org/about-us/our-mission

15   European Union, 'Key competences for lifelong learning', 2011, http://europa.eu/legislation_summaries/education_training_youth/lifelong_learning/c11090_en.htm

16   European Commission, 'The European Qualifications Framework', 2013, http://ec.europa.eu/education/lifelong-learning-policy/eqf_en.htm

17   P Hodkinson & M Issit, *The challenge of competence: professionalism through vocational education and training*, Cassell, London, 1995.

18   M Singer, 'A cognitive model for developing a competence-based curriculum in secondary education', in A Crisan (ed.), *Current and future challenges in curriculum development: policies, practices and networking for change*, Education 2000+ Publishers, Humanitas Educational, Bucharest, 2006, pp. 121–41.

19   Government of South Australia, South Australian Teaching for Effective Learning Framework guide, Department of Education and Children's Services, 2010, http://www.learningtolearn.sa.edu.au/about/files/links/DECS_TfEL_Framework__print.pdf

20   G Rodwell, 'Death by a thousand cuts. The failings of the Tasmanian essential learnings curriculum (2000–2006): the political dynamics', *Education Research and Perspectives*, vol. 36, no. 2, 2009, pp. 110–34.

21   Ministry of Education, 'Key competencies', *The New Zealand Curriculum Online*, New Zealand Government, 2007, http://nzcurriculum.tki.org.nz/Curriculum-documents/The-New-Zealand-Curriculum/Key-competencies

22   ibid.

23   Ministry of Education, 'Foreword', *The New Zealand Curriculum Online*, New Zealand Government, 2007, http://nzcurriculum.tki.org.nz/index.php/Curriculum-documents/The-New-Zealand-Curriculum/Foreword

24   Ministry of Education, 'Vision', *The New Zealand Curriculum Online*, New Zealand Government, 2007, http://nzcurriculum.tki.org.nz/index.php/Curriculum-documents/The-New-Zealand-Curriculum/Vision

25   C Isham & P Cordingley, *Opening Minds Action Research: teaching, learning and assessment on competence-based programmes*, RSA/ CUREE, London, 2012.

26   S Aynsley, C Brown & J Sebba, *Opening minds: an evaluative literature review*, RSA, London, 2012.

27   P Sahlberg, 'Education policies for raising student learning: the Finnish approach', *Journal of Education Policy*, vol. 22, no. 2, 2007, pp. 141–71.

28   Ministry of Education and Culture, 'Finnish education in a nutshell', *Education in Finland*, Espoo, 2012, http://www.minedu.fi/export/sites/ default/OPM/Julkaisut/2013/liitteet/Finnish_education_in_a_nuttshell. pdf?lang=en

29   Ministry of Education, *Desired outcomes of education*, Singapore, 2009,   http://www.moe.gov.sg/education/files/desired-outcomes-of-education.pdf

30   J Thomas, *A review of research on project-based learning*, The Autodesk Foundation, San Rafael, California, 2000, p. 1, http://www.bie.org/ research/study/review_of_project_based_learning_2000

31   A Patton, *Work that matters: the teacher's guide to project-based learning*, Paul Hamlyn Foundation, London, 2012.

32   ibid.

33   Ron Berger's ideas are persuasively set out in R Berger, *An ethic of excellence: building a culture of craftsmanship with students*, Heinemann Educational, Portsmouth, New Hampshire, 2003.

34   A Patton, op. cit.

35   ibid.

36   http://www.leonardoeffect.com/

37   Leonardo Unlimited, 'The Leonardo Effect manifesto: creative curriculum teaching', Belfast, 2011, http://www.leonardoeffect.com/ connecting_learning_to_hard_to_reach_children.html

38   http://www.shu.ac.uk/research/cse/

39   International Baccalaureate Organization, 'IB fast facts', Geneva, 2013, http://www.ibo.org/facts/fastfacts/

40   International Baccalaureate Organization, 'Mission and strategy', Geneva, 2013, http://www.ibo.org/mission/

41   C Doherty, 'Optimising meritocratic advantage with the International Baccalaureate Diploma in Australian schools', *Critical Studies in Education*, vol. 53, no. 2, 2012, pp. 183–96.

42   International Primary Curriculum, 'What is the IPC?', London, 2013, http://www.greatlearning.com/ipc/the-ipc/what-is-ipc

43   International Primary Curriculum, 'IPC learning goals', London, 2013, http://www.greatlearning.com/ipc/the-ipc/ipc-learning-goals

44   ibid.

45   ASDAN Education, 'Certificate of Personal Effectiveness (CoPE)— Levels 1 & 2', Bristol, 2013, http://www.asdan.org.uk/Qualifications/CoPE_1_and_2

46   N Harrison, D James & K Last, 'The impact of the pursuit of ASDAN's Certificate of Personal Effectiveness (CoPE) on GCSE attainment', University of the West of England & ASDAN, Bristol, 2013, http://www.asdan.org.uk/media/downloads/UWE%20report%20%20final.pdf

47   Mindset Works, 'The power of belief: mindset and success', California, 2012, http://www.mindsetworks.com/default.aspx

48   L Blackwell, K Trzesniewski & C Dweck, 'Implicit theories of intelligence predict achievement across an adolescent transition: a longitudinal study and an intervention', *Child Development*, vol. 78, 2007, pp. 246–63.

49   ibid.

50   G Claxton, *Building learning power*, TLO, Bristol, 2002.

51   G Claxton, M Chambers, G Powell & B Lucas, *The learning powered school: pioneering 21st century education*, TLO, Bristol, 2011.

52   http://www.icpic.org

53   http://www.sapere.org.uk/Default.aspx?tabid=162

54   http://www.philosophy4children.co.uk/

55   http://www.philosophy-foundation.org/home

56   See, for example, S Trickey & K Topping, 'Philosophy for Children: a systematic review', *Research Papers in Education*, vol. 19, no. 3, 2004, pp. 363–78.

57   Visible Thinking, 'Thinking routines', Project Zero, http://www.old-pz.gse.harvard.edu/vt/VisibleThinking_html_files/03_ThinkingRoutines/03a_ThinkingRoutines.html

58   http://www.thinkingschool.co.uk/creating-a-thinking-school

59   For example, http://www.thinkingschool.co.uk/pdf/thinking-skills-research-articles.pdf

60   http://expansivelearning.com.au/

61   http://www.widehorizons.org.uk/home.aspx

62   Expeditionary Learning, 'Our approach', 2012, New York, http://elschools.org/our-approach

63   Expeditionary Learning, 'Our results', 2012, New York, http://elschools.org/our-results

64   http://www.ltl.org.uk/

65   See B Lucas, 'Learning through Landscapes: an organization's attempt to move school grounds to the top of the educational agenda', *Children's Environments*, vol. 12, no. 2, 1995, pp. 233–44.

66   http://www.openfutures.com/about-open-futures/our-vision

67   D Leat, *Open Futures evaluation reports 2007–2009: summary of findings*, Open Futures, Oxford, 2009, http://www.openfutures.info/img/downloads/Evaluation_summary.pdf

68   The Eden Project, 'Learn with us', Cornwall, 2013, http://www.edenproject.com/learn-with-us

69   http://www.expansiveeducation.net/

70   http://www.lotc.org.uk/

71   http://expandedschools.org/

72   C Cummings, L Todd & A Dyson, *Evaluation of the extended schools pathfinder projects*, Department for Education and Skills, London, 2004.

73   Hands On Learning, 'About: history', Frankston, 2013, http://handsonlearning.org.au/about/history

74   Hands On Learning, 'About: evidence', Frankston, 2013, http://handsonlearning.org.au/about/our-results

75   See, for example, G Claxton, B Lucas & R Webster, *Bodies of knowledge: how the learning sciences could transform practical and vocational education*, Edge Foundation, London, 2010; B Lucas, E Spencer & G Claxton, *How to teach vocational education: a theory of vocational pedagogy*, City and Guilds Centre for Skills Development, London, 2012.

76   R Berger, *An ethic of excellence: building a culture of craftsmanship with students*, Heinemann Educational Books, Portsmouth, New Hampshire, 2003.

77   M Rose, *The mind at work: valuing the intelligence of the American worker*, Penguin Books, London, 2005.

78   M Crawford, *The case for working with your hands: or why office work is bad for us and fixing things feels good*, Penguin Books, London, 2010.

79   R Sennett, *The craftsman*, Penguin Books, London, 2009.

80   http://qedfoundation.org/

81   http://www.mc2school.org/

82   QED Foundation, 'About QED', New Hampshire, 2012, http://qedfoundation.org/about-qed/

83   QED Foundation, 'Transformational Change Model', New Hampshire, 2012, http://qedfoundation.org/transformational-change-model-2/

84   This typology can be seen in many of Epstein's extensive works. A thorough and thoughtful account can be found in E Epstein et al., *School, family and community partnerships: your handbook for action*, 3rd edn, Corwyn Press, California, 2009.

85   See, for example, A Henderson, K Mapp et al., *Beyond the bake sale: the essential guide to family/school partnerships*, The New Press, New York, 2007.

86   This chart builds on thinking in G Claxton, M Chambers, G Powell & B Lucas, *The learning powered school: pioneering 21st century education*, TLO, Bristol, 2011.

87   http://www.csos.jhu.edu/p2000/

88   http://www.hfrp.org/

89   See C Desforges & A Abouchar, *The impact of parent involvement, parent support and family education on pupil achievements and adjustment: a literature review*, Department for Education and Skills, London, 2003; A Harris & J Goodall, *Engaging parents in raising achievement: do they know they matter?* Department for Children, Schools and Families, London, 2007.

90   http://www.gemsparents.com/

91   See C Isham & P Cordingley, *Opening Minds action research: teaching, learning and assessment on competence-based programmes*, RSA & CUREE, London, 2012.

92   http://www.actionresearch.net/

93   A Lawson (ed.), Action *research: making a difference in education* (Volume 1), NFER, Slough, 2009.

94   http://acts.edublogs.org/

95   http://www.alara.net.au/public/home
96   http://www.uleth.ca/education/research/arnia
97   J Skytt, *Action research guide for Alberta teachers*, The Alberta Teachers Association, Alberta, 2000, http://www.teachers.ab.ca/ SiteCollectionDocuments/ATA/Publications/Professional-Development/ ActionResearch.pdf
98   Ofsted Inspection Report on Bay House School, 9–10 March 2011.
99   http://www.youblisher.com/p/142063-Bay-House-and-GEIP-Educational-Research-Journal-Number-2/
100   Eton College, 'Foreword', Eton, 2012, http://www.etoncollege.com/ Introduction.aspx
101   http://www.curtiscfee.org/info/

Chapter 4

1   Two pieces of research are particularly important. The first, funded by the Esmée Fairbairn Foundation, has been published as B Lucas, G Claxton & E Spencer, *Making it: studio teaching and its impact on teachers and learners*, University of Winchester, 2012. The second, funded by the City and Guilds Centre for Skills Development, is B Lucas, E Spencer & G Claxton, *How to teach vocational education: A theory of vocational pedagogy*, City and Guilds Centre for Skills Development, London, 2012.

2   J Hattie, *Visible learning for teachers: maximising impact on learning*, Routledge, London, 2012.

3   R Ritchhart, *Intellectual character: what it is, why it matters and how to get it*, Jossey-Bass, San Francisco, 2002, p. 145.

4   This phrase was coined by Anders Ericsson. See, for example, K Ericsson, R Krampe & C Tesch-Romer, 'The role of deliberate practice in the acquisition of expert performance', *Psychological Review*, vol. 100, no. 3, 1993, pp. 363–406.

5   G Claxton, B Lucas & R Webster, *Bodies of knowledge: how the learning sciences could transform practical and vocational education*, Edge Foundation, London, 2010.

6   D Perkins, *Making learning whole: how seven principles of teaching can transform education*, Jossey-Bass, San Francisco, 2009.

7   ibid.

8   E Langer, *The power of mindful learning*, Da Capo Press, New York, 1998, p. 4.

9   D Perkins, S Tishman, R Ritchhart, K Donis & A Andrade, 'Intelligence in the wild: a dispositional view of intellectual traits'. *Educational Psychology Review*, vol. 12, no. 3, 2000, pp. 269–93.

10   D Perkins & G Salomon, 'Teaching for transfer', *Educational Leadership*, vol. 46, no. 1, 1988, pp. 22–32.

11   M Csikszentmihalyi, *Flow: the psychology of optimal experience*, Harper and Row, New York, 1990.

12   M Csikszentmihalyi, *Creativity: flow and the psychology of discovery and invention*, HarperCollins, New York, 1996, p. 9.

13   L Lindström, 'Creativity. What is it? Can you assess it? Can it be taught?', *International Journal of Art & Design Education*, vol. 25, no. 1, 2006, pp. 53–66.

14   L Hetland, E Winner, S Veenema & K Sheridan, *Studio thinking: the real benefits of visual arts education*, Teachers College Press, New York, 2007.

15   R Pea, 'Practices of distributed intelligence and designs for education', in G Salomon (ed.), *Distributed cognitions: psychological and educational considerations*, Cambridge University Press, 1993, p. 81.

16   For an overview of these, see B Lucas & G Claxton, *Wider skills for learning: what are they, how can they be cultivated, how could they be measured and why are they important for innovation*, NESTA, London, 2009.

17   J Dewey, *Democracy and education*, Macmillan, New York, 1916.

18   D Boud, 'Introduction: making the move to peer learning', in D Boud, R Cohen & J Sampson (eds.), *Peer learning in higher education: learning from and with others*, Kogan Page, London, 2001, p. 3.

19   J Lave & E Wenger, *Situated learning: legitimate peripheral participation*, Cambridge University Press, 1991.

20   I Choi, S Land & A Turgeon, 'Scaffolding peer-questioning strategies to facilitate metacognition during online small group discussion', *Instructional Science*, vol. 33, no. 5–6, 2005, pp. 483–511.

21   A Bandura, *Social Learning Theory*, General Learning Press, New York, 1977, p. 22.

22   Y Sharan & S Sharan, *Expanding cooperative learning through group investigation*, Teachers College Press, New York, 1992.

23   http://www.debonothinkingsystems.com/tools/6hats.htm

24   M Frayn, *Noises Off,* 1982.

25   R Sternberg, *Intelligence applied,* Harcourt Brace Jovanovich, New York, 1986, p. 24.

26   D Perkins, *Outsmarting IQ: the emerging science of learnable intelligence,* The Free Press, New York, 1995.

27   J Hattie, *Visible learning: a synthesis of over 800 meta-analyses relating to achievement,* Routledge, London, 2009, p. 25.

28   See, for example, C Crouch & E Mazur, 'Peer instruction: ten years of experience and results', *American Journal of Physics,* vol. 69, no. 9, 2001, p. 970.

29   http://www.khanacademy.org/

30   J Savery & T Duffy, 'Problem based learning: an instructional model and its constructivist framework', *Educational Technology,* vol. 35, no. 5, 1995, pp. 31–8.

31   P Kirschner, J Sweller & R Clark, 'Why minimal guidance during instruction does not work: an analysis of the failure of constructivist, discovery, problem-based, experiential and inquiry-based teaching', *Educational Psychologist,* vol. 41, no. 2, 2006, pp. 75–86.

32   L Hetland, E Winner, S Veenema & K Sheridan, op. cit., p. 22.

33   G Claxton, M Chambers, G Powell & B Lucas, *The learning powered school: pioneering 21st century education,* TLO, Bristol, 2010.

34   The Learning Quality Framework, 'Using the framework', TLO, Bristol, 2012, http://learningqualityframework.co.uk/index.php/using-the-framework/

Chapter 5

1   M Fullan, *Choosing the wrong drivers for whole system reform,* Centre for Strategic Education Seminar series, paper no. 204, Melbourne, May, 2011, http://www.michaelfullan.com/media/13436787590.html

2   For more on theories of action, see B Lucas, *rEvolution: how to thrive in crazy times,* Crown House Publishing, Carmarthen, 2010, pp. 44–5.

3   National Teacher Research Panel, *Habitats for teacher research: teacher perspectives on research as a sustainable environment for CPD,* CUREE, Coventry, 2011, http://www.curee.co.uk/files/publication/1313750504/NTRP%20survey%20report%20FINAL_0.pdf

4   N Harrison, D James & K Last, *The impact of the pursuit of ASDAN's Certificate of Personal Effectiveness (CoPE) on GCSE attainment,*

University of the West of England, 2012, http://www.asdan.org.uk/ About_ASDAN/uwe_research_report#

5   CUREE, *QCDA: building the evidence base. Thematic synthesis report*, Coventry, 2010.

6   General Teaching Council for England, *Improving pupil learning by enhancing participation: research for teachers anthology 3*, London, 2010, http://dera.ioe.ac.uk/967/1/pupil_part_ppedg0310.pdf

7   The Leonardo Effect, 'Testimonials', Belfast, 2011, http://www. leonardoeffect.com/improving_school_performance_testimonials.html

8   V Bayliss, *Opening minds: taking stock*, Royal Society for the Encouragement of Arts, London, 2003.

9   M Bell, P Cordingley, C Isham & R Davis, *Report of professional practitioner use of research review: practitioner engagement in and/or with research*, CUREE, GTCE, LSIS & NTRP, Coventry, 2010, http:// www.curee-paccts.com/node/2303

10   ExpandED Schools, 'Why expand learning', New York, 2013, http:// w w w . e x p a n d e d s c h o o l s . o r g / w h y - e x p a n d - l e a r n i n g / close-achievement-gap

11   E Reisner, R White, C Russell & J Birmingham, *Building quality, scale, and effectiveness in after-school programs: summary report of the TASC evaluation*, Policy Studies Associates, New York, 2004, http:// www.expandedschools.org/sites/default/files/building_quality_scale_ effectiveness_afterschool_summary_0.pdf

12   ibid., p. iv.

13   ibid., p. 43.

14   ExpandED Schools, 'How we do it', New York, 2013, http://www. expandedschools.org/how-we-do-it/balanced-curriculum

15   B Lucas, G Claxton & E Spencer, *Making it: studio teaching and its impact on teachers and learners*, University of Winchester, 2012.

16   P Gollwitzer, F Wieber, A Myers & S McCrea, 'How to maximize implementation intention effects', in: C Agnew, D Carlston, W Graziano & J Kelly (eds), *Then a miracle occurs: focusing on behavior in social psychological theory and research*, Oxford University Press, New York, 2010.

17   R Zajonc, 'Attitudinal effects of mere exposure', *Journal of Personality and Social Psychology*, vol. 9, no. 2, part 2, 1968, pp. 1–27.

18   See, for example, J Sallis, R Grossman, R Pinski, T Patterson & P Nader, 'The development of scales to measure social support for diet and exercise behaviors', *Preventive Medicine*, vol. 16, no. 6, 1987, pp. 825–36.

19   L Stoll, A McMahon & S Thomas, 'Identifying and leading effective professional learning communities', *Journal of School Leadership*, vol. 16, no. 5, 2006, pp. 611–23. See also V Vescio, D Ross & A Adams, 2008, 'A review of research on the impact of professional learning communities on teaching practice and student learning', *Teaching and Teacher Education*, vol. 24, no. 1, 2008, pp. 80–91.

20   D Wiliam, 'Changing classroom practice', *Educational Leadership*, vol. 65, no. 2008, pp. 36–42.

21   P Lally, C van Jaarsveld, H Potts & J Wardle, 'How are habits formed: modelling habit formation in the real world', *European Journal of Social Psychology*, vol. 40, no. 6, 2009, pp. 998–1009.

22   D Wiliam, op. cit.

23   G Handscomb & J MacBeath, 'CPD through teacher enquiry and research', *Teaching Expertise*, May, 2008, http://www.teachingexpertise. com/articles/cpd-through-teacher-enquiry-and-research-3684

24   This section is adapted from G Claxton, M Chambers, G Powell & B Lucas, *The learning powered school: pioneering 21 century education*, TLO, Bristol, 2011.

25   C McGuiness, *From thinking skills to thinking classrooms*, Queen's University, Belfast, 1999, p. 1.

Index